Conspiracy History

Andrew May

www.BretwaldaBooks.com
@Bretwaldabooks
bretwaldabooks.blogspot.co.uk/

Bretwalda Books on Facebook

First Published 2014

Designed by Leanne Goodall

Bretwalda Books, Unit 8, Fir Tree Close, Epsom, Surrey KT17 3LD
info@BretwaldaBooks.com
www.BretwaldaBooks.com
ISBN 978-1-909698-87-1

Printed and bound in Great Britain by
Marston Book Services Ltd, Oxfordshire

Contents

Preface by Nick Redfern

There can be absolutely no doubt that in today's world of global uncertainty, conspiracy theories are everywhere: 9-11, Saddam Hussein's ever-elusive weapons of mass destruction, London's 7-7, and the Edward Snowden affair have all become targets of conspiracy theorists who believe that the stories we have been told by our elected leaders do not reflect the full facts.

Of course, there is nothing new about the idea that history as we perceive it is not necessarily how it really should be seen. One only has to look at the November 1963 assassination of United States President John F. Kennedy, the 1968 killing of Martin Luther King Jr., and NASA's Apollo moon-landings of 1969-1972 to see that widespread skepticism exists in relation to the official versions of events.

What many people may not realize, however, is that conspiracy theories are not just limited to the 20th and 21st centuries: they date back thousands of years. How do we know that? Thanks to Andrew May, that's how.

In Conspiracy History, May takes us on an illuminating, and at times shocking, ride into a world filled with lies, half-truths, high-level secrets, and official deception. The Gunpowder Plot, Jack the Ripper, the Priory of Sion, and even William Shakespeare are subjected to the May microscope.

Conspiracy History presents our world in an entirely new, and very disturbing, light.

Nick Redfern is the author of many books, including The Real Men in Black and The Pyramids and the Pentagon.

Chapter 1: A brief introduction to conspiracy theories

What is a conspiracy theory?

Conspiracy is a broad term, encompassing any clandestine plot by two or more persons to achieve an objective that could not be accomplished openly. To be of interest to a conspiracy theorist, however, the plotters must be members of the government or other powerful individuals, and the objective of the conspiracy must be to secure yet more power for the conspirators.

The appeal of conspiracy theory is obvious. There is no denying that most human beings – the powerful, ambitious ones at least – act out of self-interest, and will go to whatever lengths they can get away with to achieve their aims. For every thousand such people there may be one or two altruistic individuals who are content to act in the best interests of society... but idealists such as these were born to be trampled on. History soon forgets about them. Schemers, on the other hand, are far more interesting... so it's natural to look for them behind every major event that takes place.

The essence of conspiracy thinking can be summarized in two words: "Who benefits?" In its Latin form, *cui bono*, this phrase was popularized by the Roman politician Cicero more than two millennia ago. The Latin formula cui bono is still used in legal circles today, as a means of identifying the prime suspects in a crime investigation. But on a larger scale, what about the big events that hit our headlines every day? There are the so-called accidents and natural disasters that turn out to have far-reaching political consequences. There are the supposedly random murders and terrorist attacks that end up benefiting a third party more than they benefit the alleged perpetrators. The true conspiracy theorist is someone who applies the cui bono argument to events such as these, and adheres to the result regardless of what mainstream opinion says.

Conspiracy theorists are not always right. Sometimes things really do happen by accident, without the need for secret planning by shadowy government agencies. Or things may be planned with perfectly innocent motives and then lead to unforeseen consequences that make them look sinister in retrospect. Conspiracy theorists often underestimate the potential for incompetence that is inherent in the structure of government, particularly among middle-ranking civil servants. If the British government is discovered to have done something that runs ludicrously counter to its stated policy, for example, then it might be evidence of a conspiracy. But it is far more likely to be evidence of a cock-up.

Yet conspiracies really do occur. History is full of them, as this book will demonstrate. Strangely, however, they are not generally called conspiracies by historians. There are events that historians do refer to as conspiracies, but they're not the kind of conspiracies that conspiracy theorists are interested in.

"Caesar, beware of Brutus; take heed of Cassius; come not near Casca; have an eye to Cinna; trust not Trebonius; mark well Metellus Cimber; Decius Brutus loves thee not. There is but one mind in all these men, and it is bent against Caesar. Security gives way to conspiracy." These words are addressed to Julius Caesar in Shakespeare's play of that name. This assassination conspiracy from 44 BC is one of the most famous in history – but it was not a conspiracy in the modern sense. Julius Caesar was the dictator of Rome, and the politicians who conspired against him wanted to remove him from power. To be of interest to a conspiracy theorist, it would have to be the other way around – the dictator conspiring against his fellow politicians to keep himself in power!

Four centuries after the death of Caesar, the Roman Empire had spread across most of Europe including Britain. The oppressed locals weren't always happy about this, and the Roman military historian Ammianus Marcellinus wrote of a *barbarica conspiratio* – a Barbarian Conspiracy – against the Empire. But this was a conspiracy by the underdogs – the local British tribes – against the all-powerful Empire. While such things undoubtedly occur, they have no appeal for the hardened conspiracy theorist. On the other hand, a conspiracy by an all-powerful Empire against the enslaved masses – now that would be more like it!

"Conspiracy" used to mean a plot *against* the government – these days more often than not it means a plot *by* the government. This subtle shift in meaning has its origins in the 1960s, and to see why it is necessary to look at the mother and father of all conspiracy theories – the assassination of President John F. Kennedy in November 1963.

The JFK assassination

At the time of the assassination, the United States was locked in an international power struggle with the Soviet Union. A year earlier, the installation of Soviet nuclear missiles on the island of Cuba had brought the two superpowers to the brink of war. In November 1963, the situation was still very finely balanced. So when the U.S. President was shot dead in Dallas, the worst case scenario – in fact the most obvious scenario – was that it was the first move in a new campaign of aggression by the Soviets. The U.S. authorities, unless they were unbelievably incompetent, would need to eliminate a Soviet connection before considering

President John F. Kennedy on the day of his assassination

any alternative explanation of events.

Several gunshots were fired, and several bullets hit the President, so the first question was how many shooters there were. Careful forensic examination of the crime scene and an equally careful autopsy would be able to answer this. One alleged shooter – Lee Harvey Oswald – was under arrest. Even if he was only a minor player, he would be able to provide valuable leads. It was essential, therefore, to subject him to robust interrogation as soon as possible... and equally essential to prevent him committing suicide or otherwise being snatched from the grip of the authorities.

Astonishingly, the U.S. government didn't act like it was on the brink of nuclear war. No attempt was made to secure forensic evidence at the crime scene. The autopsy was a shambles. The chief suspect was allowed to be shot dead before he was interrogated. These are not the actions of a government that needs to find out as much as it can, as quickly as it can, in order to halt a potentially catastrophic attack by a foreign power. They are the actions of a government that already knows everything it needs to know, and wishes to keep that knowledge to itself.

The official line was that Oswald acted alone. Few people believe this, and there are countless alternative theories – far too many to go into here. However, they all share two important characteristics. First, they implicate the highest levels of U.S. government – either as being directly responsible, or as passively allowing the assassination to go ahead. Secondly, they all contradict the official view that the assassination was the work of a lone gunman. If it wasn't a lone gunman, then it was a conspiracy – hence in the most literal sense of the word the alternative hypotheses are all conspiracy theories.

Whichever way you look at it, the modern conspiracy theory was born with the JFK assassination.

Types of conspiracy theory

This isn't a book about contemporary conspiracy theories – there are enough of those already. Instead, the book looks back at historical events with the perspective of a conspiracy theorist. Whatever sinister plots are imagined to lie behind today's headlines, they all had their counterparts in the past. Each of the following chapters focuses on a different type of conspiracy, corresponding to the major preoccupations of modern-day conspiracy theorists...

False flag incidents

The term "false flag" has become popular in the last few years, to describe an operation by the government of country A, against the people of country A, purporting to be the work of country B when country B is actually innocent of any involvement. The archetypal example is the attacks of 11 September 2001 against the World Trade Center in New York. Although the attacks were blamed on terrorists, many conspiracy theorists believe they were the work of the U.S. government itself... and with hindsight the U.S. government certainly seems to have gained more from the incident than the alleged terrorist perpetrators have. Whether 9/11 was a false flag operation or not, such operations have occurred repeatedly throughout history – as we will see in Chapter 2.

They acted alone – or did they?

The official narrative of the JFK assassination is the archetypal example of the "lone gunman" scenario. A supposedly deranged individual carries out an act which ends up benefiting himself not at all, while other more powerful figures – who manage to keep their hands clean – benefit a great deal. But JFK is simply the best known victim of the lone (or not so lone) assassin – many others can be found in Chapter 3.

Hidden agendas

Not all conspiracy theories deal with situations where the government denies any involvement in the events in question. Sometimes the issue is one of motive. When the U.S. and its allies invaded Iraq in 2003, did they do so for the stated reason – due to concerns over Iraq's (non-existent, as it turned out) weapons of mass destruction? Or was it for some other reason, connected perhaps with the state of Israel and/or the international oil industry? Hidden agendas of this kind are nothing new, as Chapter 4 will reveal.

Convenient deaths

When Diana Princess of Wales died in a car crash in 1997, it might have been an accident. But it was an accident that came as a huge relief to the British Royal Family, for whom Diana had been a dangerously loose cannon for years. To conspiracy theorists, this is too much of a coincidence. Important people – particularly ones that other important people want dead – don't just die in random accidents. All-too-convenient accidents of this type have cropped up time and again throughout history, as Chapter 5 will show.

Secret identities

Perhaps the most bizarre of all contemporary conspiracy theories is the idea that the British Royal Family – the ones who so desperately wanted Diana dead – are not human beings at all but members of a sinister race of shape-shifting reptilians. While this particular belief is probably too far-fetched to be true, there's no doubt that certain people throughout history have been something other than they appear to be. A range of secret identities will be divulged in Chapter 6.

The Illuminati and others

One of the major themes of conspiracy theorists is the New World Order – the idea that a powerful, secret elite is working on a level above national governments to reshape the world for its own nefarious purposes. The idea that true world power lies in the hands of exclusive secret societies is nothing new – the Illuminati and others are discussed in Chapter 7.

Rewriting history

Most of what we know about history comes from the written word... but can you trust what has been written? There is an insidious trend at the moment towards holocaust denial – the idea that the Nazi persecution of the Jews during the 1930s and 40s never took place. Holocaust deniers are the latest in a long line of people who have attempted to rewrite history – we'll encounter some of their predecessors in Chapter 8.

All Seeing Eye on US Dollar bill.

Chapter 2: False flag incidents

False flag operations of the Cold War (1961-64)

Throughout the 1950s and 60s, the United States was in a state of collective paranoia about the spread of Communism. The country was locked in a Cold War with the Soviet Union, which at the time was the most powerful Communist country in the world. The Americans didn't want a war with the Soviets, because they weren't sure they could win. But they were itching for war against some of Russia's less powerful Communist allies. The problem was, any act of overt aggression against such countries was likely to trigger an unwelcome response from the Soviets. So America was forced to turn to more devious methods.

The island of Cuba lies less than a hundred miles from the U.S. coast. In 1959, following the revolution led by Fidel Castro, it became a fully fledged Communist state and a staunch ally of the Soviet Union. The Americans didn't like that, and they knew they had the military capability to invade Cuba and return it to non-Communist hands. But they had to find a way of doing it that wouldn't escalate into a war with Russia. In short, America had to invade Cuba and make it look like someone else was responsible. The result was the Bay of Pigs fiasco.

In the early hours of 15 April 1961, eight B-26 bombers mounted simultaneous attacks on airbases across Cuba. The aircraft were owned and operated by America's Central Intelligence Agency, but they bore the "false flag" markings of the Cuban Air Force and were ostensibly flown by Cuban rebels unhappy with the country's Communist government. The air raids were just the first step – they were followed two days later by a major amphibious invasion at a place called the Bay of Pigs. That, too, was purportedly carried out by Cuban rebels while being secretly masterminded by the CIA. Fortunately for Castro's government – and unfortunately for America – the invasion was a dismal failure, and the role of the United States became public knowledge almost immediately.

Less than a year later, in March 1962, the CIA in collaboration with the Joint Chiefs of Staff proposed an even more audacious plot against Cuba's Communist government. Instead of attacking Communists, this time they would attack Americans. One small part of the island of Cuba, around Guantanamo Bay, was not in Communist hands – it had been U.S. territory since the end of the 19th century. The new scheme, called Operation Northwoods, was simple but devious. To quote from the proposal itself, "A series of well coordinated incidents will be planned to take place in and around Guantanamo to give genuine appearance of being done by hostile Cuban forces".

The proposal gives a number of specific examples of what might be done, such as "We could blow up a U.S. ship in Guantanamo Bay and blame Cuba." That is a direct quote from an official U.S. government document! Needless to say, the document was marked Top Secret, and was only released to the public in 1997... ironically for conspiracy theorists, in the context of the John F. Kennedy Assassination Records Review Board.

Operation Northwoods was never put into effect, but similar Machiavellian thinking appears to have been behind the Gulf of Tonkin Resolution which effectively started the Vietnam War. Passed by Congress on 7 August 1964, this gave President Lyndon B. Johnson authority to use whatever military force was necessary to halt the spread of Communism in South-East Asia. The name of the resolution comes from two incidents that supposedly took place in the Gulf of Tonkin a few days earlier, on 2 and 4 August, when North Vietnamese torpedo boats launched unprovoked attacks on U.S. Navy ships. The U.S. media were outraged at the incident and demanded action, and the Gulf of Tonkin Resolution was the almost immediate response.

Virtually all historians agree that the "attack" of 4 August never took place at all, while the earlier attack was deliberately provoked by the Americans who fired the first shots. In other words, the Gulf of Tonkin Resolution was predicated on a pair of lies... but it was enough to propel the United States into one of the longest and bloodiest wars in its history.

The Nazis and Operation Himmler (1939)

The Second World War was triggered by a single event – the invasion of Poland by Nazi Germany on 1 September 1939. Ostensibly, this was a legitimate act of self-defence – a response to Polish aggression against Germany. But in reality there was no such aggression – it was a classic case of a False Flag operation. Just over a week before the invasion, on 22 August 1939, Hitler told his military commanders: "The start of the conflict will be accomplished through suitable propaganda. Its credibility is immaterial, its legality lies in victory."

The plan was the brainchild of the notorious Reichsführer-SS Heinrich Himmler, and historians refer to it as Operation Himmler for that reason. Dozens of attacks were carried out by the SS and other German troops, dressed in Polish uniforms, against German targets along the border with Poland. Dead bodies, also dressed in Polish uniforms, were left behind with suitably convincing bullet wounds. But in reality the victims had been dead for some time – inmates of concentration camps who had been killed by lethal injection. With characteristic heartlessness, the Nazis referred to such bodies as "canned meat".

The best known of the Operation Himmler attacks was the Gleiwitz Incident, which took place on 31 August 1939 when Nazi soldiers posing as Polish saboteurs took over a German radio station at Gleiwitz in Silesia. The "saboteurs" broadcast a message in Polish, and left behind a few canned-meat bodies – including a well-known dissident named Franciszek Honiok who had been captured and executed the previous day.

All this Polish aggression was too much for Hitler... despite the fact that he had authorized it himself. In a speech to the German parliament the day after the Gleiwitz Incident, he said "I am wrongly judged if my love of peace and my patience are mistaken for weakness or even cowardice. I therefore decided last night and informed the British Government that in these circumstances I can no longer find any willingness on the part of the Polish Government to conduct serious negotiations with us. These proposals for mediation have failed because there came as an answer the sudden Polish general mobilization, followed by more Polish atrocities. These were again repeated last night. Recently in one night there were as many as twenty-one frontier incidents: last night there were fourteen, of which three were quite serious. I have, therefore, resolved to speak to Poland in the same language that Poland for months past has used toward us." This was a declaration of war – a war against an aggressor that didn't exist!

Heinrich Himmler

The Reichstag Fire (1933)

On 27 February 1933 a young Dutch Communist named Marinus van der Lubbe set fire to the German parliament building, the Reichstag, in Berlin. Van der Lubbe claimed he was acting alone, as a protest against the government, but many people saw his actions as part of a wider Communist plot. Among them was the recently appointed Chancellor of Germany, Adolf Hitler, who used the Reichstag Fire as an excuse to clamp down on Communists and remove them from Parliament. In so doing, he ensured a comfortable majority for his own Nazi party, thus paving the way for the establishment of the Third Reich.

So the Communists caused the Reichstag Fire, yet their mortal enemies the Nazis reaped the benefits of it. Does that make sense? Not to a Conspiracy Theorist it doesn't! It's far more likely that the fire was started on the orders of Hitler himself, with the deliberate intention of framing the Communists... a scenario that even mainstream historians are beginning to accept.

The Sinking of the Lusitania (1915)

The RMS *Lusitania* was launched by Cunard in 1907. At 32,000 tons she was one of the largest passenger ships of the time, becoming a regular on the lucrative transatlantic route between Liverpool and New York. By April 1915, some nine months after the outbreak of the First World War, the *Lusitania* had completed no less than 200 Atlantic crossings.

Britain was one of the countries fighting the war. British ships like the *Lusitania* were prey to German U-boats, particularly in the waters around the British Isles which Germany had declared to be a War Zone. The United States remained neutral in the war, but was happy to supply Britain with arms and ammunition – transported across the Atlantic on whatever ships had space in their holds.

The Sinking of the *Lusitania* (1915)

When the *Lusitania* arrived in New York on 24 April at the end of her 201st transatlantic crossing, she was duly loaded up with shells, machine gun ammo and other explosives in addition to almost 2,000 passengers and crew. Of the passengers, 139 were U.S. citizens – many more Americans had been deterred from travelling by a notice the German embassy had placed in newspapers warning that the ship was a legitimate target for their submarines.

On the last day of the return trip – 7 May 1915 – when the *Lusitania* was less than a day away from docking in Liverpool, she was torpedoed by a German U-boat near the coast of Ireland. The huge liner sank almost immediately, with the death of more than a thousand people – including 128 of the 139 Americans on board. In light of the German warnings, this tragic outcome seems all but inevitable.

Why did the British allow the *Lusitania* to sail, without an armed escort, through the very waters the Germans had declared to be a War Zone? There are only two possible answers – either the government was grossly incompetent, or they knew exactly what they were doing. Most conspiracy theorists would put their money on the second of these. Britain didn't like the fact that America was remaining neutral in the war – they wanted to see Americans fighting alongside them against the Germans. An atrocity like the sinking of a civilian liner was just the sort of thing that could swing American public opinion in their favour. Shortly before the sinking of the *Lusitania*, Winston Churchill – who at the time was First Lord of the Admiralty – had written to another minister that it was "most important to attract neutral shipping to our shores, in the hope especially of embroiling the United States with Germany." Translating from the deliberately obscure phraseology of the professional politician, this boils down to "the sooner an innocent ship gets sunk, the sooner the Americans will join us in the trenches".

As it turned out, the ruse – if it was a ruse – was not immediately successful. Instead of joining the war, the Americans secured a promise from the German government that an incident such as the sinking of the *Lusitania* wouldn't happen again. It was only when the Germans withdrew this promise, early in 1917, that the United States finally decided it was time to go to war.

Remember the Maine! (1898)

In 1895 Cuba embarked on a war of independence against Spain. Alarmed at the prospect of Spanish military action so close to its own shores, the United States despatched one of its largest battleships, the USS *Maine*, to the Cuban capital Havana in January 1898. The aim was not to get involved in any fighting, but simply to sit in port as a show of strength – "in order to impress upon the Spanish authorities the seriousness with which our government, and indeed the whole American people, view the situation," as an official in Washington wrote at the time.

Three weeks after the *Maine* arrived in Havana, on the evening of 15 February, she was torn apart by a huge explosion. The ship sank to the bottom of the harbour, killing some 260 people of the 350-odd on board. A subsequent inquiry suggested the explosion had been caused by a submerged mine – but who planted the mine, and why?

For many Americans, the answer was obvious. Spain was America's enemy, and a war with Spain was long overdue. The Spanish had sunk the USS *Maine*, and they needed to be punished for it. A rallying cry went up – "Remember the *Maine*! To Hell with Spain!" Public opinion was so outraged that the Spanish-American War broke out just two months after the sinking, with the United States emerging victorious after three months of fighting.

But is it really credible that Spain sank a US battleship that posed no obvious threat to its interests? The only foreseeable consequence of doing so was the very thing that happened – a war against a much better equipped enemy. And was the explosion really caused by a mine? The physical evidence suggested the explosion took place inside the ship's hull, not outside. It is far more likely that the sinking of the *Maine* was a False Flag operation by the United States – with the deliberate aim of shifting public opinion in favour of a war against Spain. For most people, this is just another conspiracy theory – but for the Communist government of Cuba it is nothing less than the truth. In 1961 they altered the wording on a monument to the victims of the *Maine*, which the Americans had erected in Havana in 1926. It now reads "To the victims of the *Maine* who were sacrificed by imperialist voracity in its eagerness to seize the island of Cuba".

Bismarck's war (1870)

Prussia was a powerful country, and part of what became the even more powerful country of Germany. In fact it was a Prussian Prime Minister, Otto von Bismarck, who originally unified Germany in 1871. This was the culmination of Bismarck's grand plan, and before he could achieve it he needed to do a few other things as well. One of them was to start a war between France and Prussia... but he had to make it look like the war was started by France. That was the only way he could persuade the allies he needed to join in with his plan.

Some of the groundwork for war had already been laid. There was tension between King Wilhelm of Prussia and Emperor Napoleon III of France over a number of matters – but unfortunately for Bismarck they insisted on resolving their differences amicably, without recourse to war. For example when a German prince, Leopold of Hohenzollern, was offered the Spanish crown, the French Emperor objected on the grounds that it would give the Germans too much power. Leopold graciously agreed to decline the offer – which was bad news for Bismarck because it averted the war he was trying to start.

Then another opportunity presented itself. On 13 July 1870, Bismarck learned that the French Ambassador had approached King Wilhelm, while the latter was on vacation at a bathing resort called Ems, with a new proposal. The Frenchman suggested, in polite diplomatic language, that it would be really rather nice if the Prussian King would promise that a Hohenzollern candidate would never again be put forward as a contender for the Spanish throne. The King, equally politely, declined to do this on the perfectly reasonable grounds that he never said never.

When the account of the conversation was passed to Bismarck, as the King's Prime Minister, he was given permission to release it to the press. He did this, but not before he'd made subtle adjustments to the wording. In Bismarck's version, the French Ambassador had made strident demands of the King, to which the King had replied in a way that insulted not only the Ambassador but the French Emperor as well. Just as Bismarck hoped, this "Ems Despatch", as it became known, inflamed French public opinion against the Prussians. Its effect was heightened by the fact that it was published on 14 July – Bastille Day, the most important day in the French calendar.

Five days later, on 19 July 1870, France declared war on Prussia. Bismarck's plan was coming together – and it continued to do so, with victory over France and the final unification of Germany following soon afterwards.

Costume drama (1788)

King Gustav III of Sweden was an unpopular and autocratic leader who seized power in a coup d'état in 1772. He needed to get the country behind him, and what better way to do so than to start a war with Russia? Unfortunately, the constitution only allowed him to declare war on a country in self-defence, after Sweden had been attacked. But that's no great problem – at least, not for someone who has mastered the art of the False Flag operation.

On 27 June 1788, Swedish society was outraged by news of an unprovoked attack against a border outpost by troops dressed in Russian uniforms. The king was incensed too – he declared war on the Russians without delay.

And where does the false flag come in? Just a few days earlier the costume department of the Royal Swedish Opera in Stockholm received a large anonymous order – for Russian military uniforms!

The Popish Plot (1678)

During the 16th and 17th centuries, European politics was dominated by the rift between Catholics and Protestants. England was a Protestant country, and the Civil War in the middle of the 17th century saw the rise of a strongly anti-Catholic movement called Puritanism. After the restoration of King Charles II in 1660, however, there was a shift towards religious tolerance among higher levels of the establishment. The King himself was married to a Catholic, Catherine of Braganza, while his brother – the future James II – was also a Catholic.

Further down the chain, Puritanical intolerance and anti-Catholic sentiment were still the order of the day. Many people felt the King was too soft on Catholics, and that they ought to be expelled from the country altogether. One such extremist was a paranoid individual named Israel Tonge, who had been rector of a church that was burnt down during the Great Fire of London in 1666. Tonge openly blamed Catholic priests for starting the fire.

In 1678, Tonge teamed up with an unlikely ally – a young man named Titus Oates who had been expelled from a Catholic college in France. Though his reasons were quite different, Oates hated the Catholics almost as much as Tonge did. Between them, they hatched a plot – a kind of private enterprise false flag operation – that they hoped would persuade the King to outlaw Catholicism once and for all.

The essence of the Popish Plot, as it became known, was that a group of powerful Catholics –including the Queen's personal physician and possibly even the Queen herself – were conspiring to assassinate the King. Over the course of weeks extensive evidence came to light... all of it fabricated by Oates, Tonge and various members of the criminal underworld they persuaded to join them.

To give greater credence to their allegations, Oates and Tonge agreed to swear an oath before a magistrate. The magistrate in question was named Edmund Berry Godfrey, and on 28 September 1678 he duly took their depositions. Less than three weeks later, Godfrey was found face down in a ditch on Primrose Hill. He had been strangled, his neck was broken, and he had been run through with his own sword. Three Catholic priests were executed for the murder, but – apart from the fact they were Catholics – there was no material evidence against them. It seems far more likely the murder was the work of Oates and Tonge themselves – either as a random killing to frame the Catholics, or because Godfrey was on the point of exposing their fraudulent activities.

To his credit, the King never really believed in the Popish Plot – he considered Tonge to be a madman and Oates a liar. Most people disagreed with him, however, and a period of anti-Catholic hysteria followed. No fewer than 24 Catholics were falsely accused of treason and executed between December 1678 and July 1681. Israel Tonge and Titus Oates became national heroes, and were granted state apartments in Whitehall together with generous salaries. It all came to an abrupt end in September 1681, however. By this time Tonge had died a natural death, while

Oates was becoming increasingly outrageous in his accusations – even hinting that the King himself was part of the plot to kill the King. Oates was charged with sedition and thrown into jail... a relatively lenient punishment for someone with so much blood on his hands!

The Gunpowder Plot (1605)

The Gunpowder Plot of 1605 is one of the best known events in English history. It's so well known, in fact, that few people look beyond the conventional narrative to see if there is more to the "plot" than meets the eye.

The basic facts are clear enough. Towards the end of October, a junior member of the House of Lords named Baron Monteagle received an anonymous letter warning him to stay away from the State Opening of Parliament on 5 November. Unsure of what the letter meant, Monteagle passed it on to the Earl of Salisbury, who was the King's Secretary of State. In turn, Salisbury showed the letter to the King himself – James I, who had acceded to the throne two years earlier. The King interpreted the letter to mean that an attack would be made on the House of Lords, which was duly searched. In the early hours of 5 November, a man named Guy Fawkes was found lurking in the basement, together with enough gunpowder to destroy the House of Lords and everyone inside it.

It soon emerged that Fawkes was just one member of the plot, which had been the work of a group of Catholics intent on removing the Protestants from power and installing a Catholic monarch instead. In fact, with the exposure of their plot, the ultimate effect was the opposite of what they had hoped for. More stringent anti-Catholic legislation was introduced, collective paranoia against Catholicism intensified, and the previously unpopular King's approval rating soared through the roof.

Although the Gunpowder Plot was a conspiracy in the dictionary sense of the word, it did not immediately give rise to "conspiracy theories" in the modern sense. Before the 17th century

The Gunpowder Plot

was over, however, the situation changed. With the revelation that the Popish Plot of the 1670s and 80s had been a hoax, people started to wonder if the same was true of the Gunpowder Plot. There were striking similarities – both plots involved supposed attempts by Catholics to assassinate a Protestant monarch, and both had resulted in worse, rather than better, conditions for Catholics.

There were differences, however. In the case of the Popish Plot, the accused Catholics were entirely innocent of the charges against them. That wasn't the case with the Gunpowder Plot. Guy Fawkes and his fellow conspirators really were Catholics, and they really did want to blow up Parliament, kill the King and replace the Protestant establishment with a Catholic one. But who gave them the idea?

Conspiracy theories often target Lord Salisbury, whose public role in the Gunpowder Plot was much the same as that of Titus Oates in the Popish Plot 75 years later. Salisbury was the one who exposed the alleged conspiracy to the world, and he was the one who went on to foil it like a blue-blooded English hero. Does this mean that, like Titus Oates, Salisbury was the real architect of the conspiracy... who somehow contrived to put it in the minds of the Catholic rebels? If that sounds too far-fetched, there is another possibility. It's much more likely that Salisbury discovered the

Catholic plot weeks or months before it was put into effect, and allowed it to go ahead so he could jump in and foil it at the last minute!

Entrapment of a Queen (1587)

Mary Queen of Scots was executed by beheading on 8 February 1587, on the orders of Queen Elizabeth I of England. The two queens were long-time rivals – Mary was a Catholic and Elizabeth was a Protestant. Elizabeth had kept Mary prisoner for almost 20 years, since 1568, but she needed a more permanent solution. Eventually, the perfect opportunity presented itself. A coded letter was intercepted from Mary to Anthony Babington, a young Englishman who was plotting a Catholic revolution that would begin with the assassination of Queen Elizabeth. In the letter, Mary gave her unequivocal support to both the assassination and the revolution. This was a clear case of treason, and all the excuse Elizabeth needed to execute Mary.

While the earnest young Babington was perfectly serious in his plans, there was a small detail he was unaware of. Virtually all his co-conspirators were members of the English court – double-agents loyal to Elizabeth. They were working to a completely different agenda from Babington himself. There was no way they were going to allow the assassination or subsequent revolution to go ahead – they simply needed Mary to believe it would. The real purpose of the plot was to get Mary to incriminate herself!

Chapter 3:
They acted alone - or did they?

The assassination of Abraham Lincoln (1865)

Assassination of President Lincoln

Abraham Lincoln was the first President of the United States to be assassinated, almost a century before John F. Kennedy. There are striking parallels between the two events, but there are also important differences. In the case of JFK, the official version of events is adamant that the assassin acted alone. With Lincoln, however, there is no doubt that some form of conspiracy was involved. The question is whether this was a conspiracy by relatively unimportant people with trivial grievances – as the official account would have it – or whether the conspiracy went to the highest levels of American government.

Lincoln was assassinated on 14 April 1865, as the Confederate States were on the point of surrendering at the end of the four year long American Civil War. It happened in the evening, as Lincoln and his wife were attending a theatre performance in Washington D.C. The assassin was an actor named John Wilkes Booth, who forced his way into Lincoln's box and shot the President in the back of the head, before jumping onto the stage with a cry of "The South is avenged!"

Booth made his escape, but was later caught and killed. A number of co-conspirators were identified, all of them low-ranking Confederate sympathizers like Booth himself, and were duly executed. The official verdict of history is that the conspirators were simple-minded southerners motivated by a poorly articulated grievance against the Union. Seen in context, however, this seems improbable. The assassination occurred at a critical point in U.S. history, when the whole future of the country was hanging in the balance. The Civil War was not yet formally over, and the stakes couldn't have been higher.

Following Lincoln's assassination, the Presidency passed to Vice President Andrew Johnson. One of Johnson's first acts was to accuse the Confederate leader Jefferson Davis of masterminding the assassination, offering a $100,000 reward for his capture. Davis, however, was dismayed at Lincoln's assassination – or rather, he was dismayed at the fact that Andrew Johnson was now the President. Davis knew he'd lost the Civil War, and he would have much preferred to deal with Lincoln, who was known for his intelligence and integrity, than with the hard-hitting Johnson.

So what about Johnson himself? Based on the *cui bono* ("who benefits?") argument, he's the obvious suspect – he gained more than anyone else from the assassination. Despite being on Lincoln's side in the Civil War, he was a southerner by birth – so he could easily have infiltrated groups of Confederate supporters even if he didn't agree with their views. He might simply have been using them as pawns to further his own interests.

There is one very damning piece of evidence against Johnson. After the assassination, it emerged that the assassin had visited Johnson's hotel earlier in the day. Johnson wasn't in at the time, but Booth left a card in his in-box with the message: "I don't wish to disturb you. Are you at home? J. Wilkes Booth." The implication that Booth and Johnson were acquaintances is difficult to escape. If Booth had been unknown to Johnson, why would he leave such a message – for one of the most important people in the country – without explaining who he was or what he wanted to discuss?

Lincoln's widow Mary certainly believed that Johnson was in on the plot. In a letter written to a friend a year after the assassination, she wrote: "That miserable inebriate Johnson had cognizance of my husband's death. Why was that card of Booth's found in his box? Some acquaintance certainly existed. I have been deeply impressed with the harrowing thought that he had an understanding with the conspirators and they knew their man. As sure as you and I live, Johnson had some hand in all this."

The welcome demise of a Prime Minister (1812)

No fewer than four U.S. Presidents have been assassinated, but only one British Prime Minister has suffered the same fate. This was Spencer Perceval, who was shot dead in the crowded lobby of the House of Commons on 11 May 1812. British readers will be unsurprised to learn that, when the news hit the streets that the Prime Minister had been killed, there was unrestrained jubilation the length and breadth of the country. Prime Ministers are almost never popular – being blamed for whatever woes the country is suffering at the time. In the case of Perceval, the woes in question were particularly severe, due to the expensive and long-running war against the Emperor Napoleon.

Napoleon came to power in the wake of the French Revolution, and the British upper classes were terrified of the prospect of an English Revolution along similar lines. Some people feared the Prime Minister's assassination was the first move in such a

The assassination of Prime Minister Spencer Perceval.

revolution. However, it soon became clear that the assassin – a middle-aged businessman named John Bellingham – was acting out a private vendetta of his own. He made no secret of his grievances, and took every opportunity to air them. After the shooting, the authorities were slow to arrive on the scene, but Bellingham made no attempt to escape. He sat down on a bench and waited for them – there were important matters he wanted to explain to them. He was equally forthcoming at his trial, and again when he was standing on the scaffold as the hangman placed the rope around his neck. He wanted the world to know how he had been cheated out of every penny he owned by some Russian fraudsters, and how the Prime Minister had refused to aid him financially when he requested it.

At first sight, from the point of view of a Conspiracy Theorist, the case looks disappointing. It's clear that Bellingham believed he was acting alone... and acting solely in his own interests, which were almost comically trivial. Looking a bit deeper, however, there is a mystery that needs to be explained. Bellingham, as he never tired of telling anyone who would listen, had lost every penny. Yet for several months prior to the assassination he was living in comfortable lodgings in London, with every display of affluence. Where was his money coming from? He certainly didn't have a legitimate income at the time, since his only "employment" was to lobby the Prime Minister on a daily basis and threaten him with drastic action if his demands weren't met.

There were other people who wanted Spencer Perceval dead. One of his more draconian measures against the French took the form of a commercial embargo... which threatened to be just as damaging to certain British and American businessmen as it was to the French. It's possible that one or more such businessmen heard Bellingham threatening to kill the Prime Minister, and decided to subsidise him financially in the hope that he would carry out his threat. If so, then Bellingham's anonymous sponsors benefited far more than he did himself – Perceval's successor promptly cancelled the embargo and the British economy experienced a sharp upturn.

The trial of the century (1616)

The most sensational trial of the 17th century took place in London in 1616. It was a murder trial, and the victim was a man named Thomas Overbury. At the time of his death, Overbury was in what should, in principle, have been one of the safest locations in the country. He was a prisoner inside the Tower of London – not the sort of place one might reasonably expect to be murdered. He had been imprisoned by King James I in April 1613, for refusing an order to take up an ambassadorial position abroad. Soon after he was incarcerated Overbury developed a serious illness, which got progressively worse. Six months later, in September 1613, he was found dead in his cell.

Initially the death – and indeed the illness – were assumed to have natural causes. But two years later, the Governor of the Tower of London received an anonymous tip-off which led him to look more carefully at the circumstances surrounding Overbury's death. It soon became clear that foul play had been involved –

someone had slowly and methodically poisoned Overbury to death. But how had that happened, inside the most secure prison in the country?

Gradually a complex web of intrigue was unravelled, and no fewer than six people were charged with Overbury's murder. Two of the defendants, Jervis Elwes and Richard Weston, were prison officials who were accused of supplementing the victim's diet with an unhealthy dose of poison. The third defendant, Simon Franklin, was an apothecary who had prepared the alleged poison, while the fourth was a "woman of ill repute", Anne Turner, who had passed the concoction on to Elwes and Weston. But these four were low-ranking members of society who wouldn't normally attract the attention of the public or the media. What made the trial the juiciest scandal of its day were the remaining two defendants – high-ranking members of the King's inner circle named Robert and Frances Carr.

The Carrs were married in December 1613, soon after the death of Overbury. The latter had been a former friend of Robert Carr who was vociferously opposed to the marriage – it seems he knew unsavoury facts about both Robert and Frances that he was going to make public if the marriage went ahead. It was Robert Carr who had suggested that it would be a good idea if the King gave Overbury an ambassadorship in a distant country... and then encouraged James to lock him up when the man refused. But locking him up wasn't enough to silence him – Overbury continued to write threatening letters to Robert and Frances after he was consigned to the Tower. So they were forced to resort to murder.

All six of the accused were found guilty of murder, and all six were sentenced to death. But the sentence was only carried out in the case of the first four. Due to the intervention of the King, Robert and Frances Carr had their sentences commuted to life imprisonment. And the King's generosity didn't stop there – six years later, in 1622, the two of them were released from prison with a full royal pardon.

The question conspiracy theorists will be asking is why King James I was so accommodating to the Carrs. Why did he agree to jail Overbury in the first place, and why did he let Robert and Frances off with such light sentences? The answer is almost certainly that James – who like Robert was bisexual – found himself in exactly the same predicament. Overbury had dirt on the King and was threatening to make it public!

Murder at the masked ball (1792)

The last time we met King **Gustav III** of Sweden, he was organizing a False Flag operation against the Russians with the ostensible aim of making himself more popular with the Swedish. The ruse didn't work – the war was indecisive and Gustav remained as unpopular as ever. During dinner on the evening of 16 March 1792 he was handed an anonymous letter threatening him with assassination. He ignored it – he was used to receiving death threats.

Later that night there was a masked ball, which the King attended. Although his face was covered by a mask, he was easily identifiable because he was still wearing his royal regalia. Almost as soon as he entered the room he was surrounded by three men in black masks, one of whom shot Gustav in the back – a fitting end for the scheming monarch.

Years later, in 1859, the Italian composer Giuseppe Verdi wrote an opera about the assassination that was originally entitled *Gustavo III*. But the censors didn't like the idea of an opera showing the assassination of a King – it might stir up revolutionary ideas. Verdi was forced to transfer the action to 17th century Boston, giving Gustav's role to an autocratic British governor. Confusingly, the opera – now entitled *Un Ballo in Maschera* – is sometimes performed with an American setting and sometimes with a Swedish one!

The Queen's lucky day (1610)

17th century France was a hotbed of religious paranoia just as much as 17th century England was, and equally divided along Catholic-Protestant lines. The man who was later to become Henri IV was born in Catholic France, but he was raised in the small Protestant country of Navarre. Henri became king of Navarre at the age of 19 in 1572. A few months later he was one of the primary targets of the St Bartholomew Day's Massacre, which saw the murder of numerous high-ranking French Protestants. Henri only escaped with his life after promising he would convert back to Catholicism.

Henri wasn't in any hurry to keep his promise. However, by 1593 – more than 20 years later – the stakes had been raised. By this time, he had nominally inherited the French throne, but as a Protestant there was no way he was going to be allowed to rule the country. If he became a Catholic, on the other hand... Henri decided to take a pragmatic approach. Reputedly saying "Paris is worth a Mass", he converted back to Catholicism – and was duly crowned Henri IV of France a few months later.

Not surprisingly, Henri had no shortage of enemies. Protestants saw him as an out-and-out traitor, while Catholics felt he was a duplicitous cynic who only paid lip-service to their cause. He survived at least two assassination attempts before the final, successful one. This took place on 14 May 1610 – the day following the coronation of his second wife, Marie de' Medici, as Queen of France. The King's carriage was forced to stop due to a blockage caused by two carts, one carrying wine and the other hay. At this point, the assassin François Ravaillac leapt up and stabbed the King to death.

The death of Henri IV

The official view – and this is going to sound familiar – was that the assassination was the work of a fanatic who acted alone. This theory, however, poses more questions than it answers. How could Ravaillac possibly know in advance that the road would be blocked at just that point? Why did the authorities make no attempt to clear the streets ahead of the King's procession? Even under extreme torture Ravaillac swore that he had no accomplices... but this only proves one thing. His torturers wanted him to swear that he had no accomplices. Torture doesn't extract the truth, it extracts whatever message the interrogators want to hear.

If Ravaillac wasn't acting alone, who was really behind the assassination? As usual, we can look to see who benefited the most from the King's death. The obvious answer is his successor – but his successor was his son, Louis XIII, who was only eight years old at the time of his father's death. Even the most fervent conspiracy theorist wouldn't pin an assassination on an eight year old!

Because Louis was so young, the country was ruled on his behalf by his mother, Marie de' Medici. By an odd coincidence – if it was a coincidence – the assassination just happened to take place a day after she was crowned Queen of France. It was her lucky day! While publicly lamenting her husband's death, she clearly relished her new found power... as did a number of her close advisors. As a native of Italy, she was a much stronger Catholic than Henri had been, and she raised her son in the same tradition. So anyone who subscribes to the *cui bono* school of conspiracy theories need look no further than Marie, or someone very close to her, for the true instigator of her husband's murder.

The man with the red-hot poker (1327)

Edward I was one of the strongest of the mediaeval English kings. The same could not be said of his son, Edward II, who inherited the throne on his father's death in 1307. The country's fortunes took a sudden nose dive, with military blunders and disastrous decisions becoming the order of the day. The king's French-born wife, Isabella, became convinced she could do a much better job of running the country than her dismally incompetent husband. Joining forces with one of Edward's long-time enemies, a man named Roger Mortimer, she launched a coup d'état.

Edward responded to the coup in the only way he knew how – by suffering a humiliating defeat. Isabella forced him to abdicate the crown in favour of their son, who formally became King Edward III on 24 January 1327. But the boy was only 14, so his mother generously offered to rule the country in his place – aided and abetted, of course, by Roger Mortimer.

There was still a loose end to tie up – what was to be done with ex-King Edward II? He was imprisoned at Berkeley Castle in Gloucestershire, in the care of two of Mortimer's loyal followers named Thomas Gournay and William Oakley. Presumably these men were given orders by Mortimer and Isabella, although the details of such orders have been lost to history. One can only infer their nature from the way subsequent events unfolded.

On the night of 21 September 1327, horrible screams were heard emanating from Edward's cell. The following morning he was found dead. A doctor who was called to the scene found no obvious cause of death, and he was happy to go along with the suggestion that the ex-King had died of natural causes.

The consensus of history is different – almost everyone agrees that Edward was murdered by Gournay and Oakley. There is no agreement on the exact technique used, however. Some of the earliest reports suggest strangling or suffocation, but these would have left tell-tale signs on the body that the doctor would have recognised. From the 1340s onwards, one phrase crops up time and again in accounts of Edward's demise – "red-hot poker". But wouldn't such an implement leave marks on the body that even the most incompetent medic would notice? Not if the job is done properly: "They pinioned him with legs spread and a kind of horn or funnel was thrust into his fundament through which a red-hot spit was run up his bowels".

With Edward II out of the picture, the way was clear for Mortimer and Isabella to rule the country together. Unfortunately for them, young Edward III proved to have a shrewder mind than his father. By the time he was 17, he had worked out pretty much what was going on. He declared Mortimer a traitor and had him hung, drawn and quartered. For the young king, that was the end of it – he saw Mortimer as the sole villain of the piece. Other people knew better.

Gournay and Oakley – the two men who knew the facts about Edward II's murder – were sentenced to death. But Gournay escaped, and succeeded in fleeing to the continent. He was pursued by two groups of people – agents of the King who wanted to bring him back to England to face justice, and agents of Isabella who wanted to silence him as soon as possible. Gournay was tracked first to Spain and then to Italy, where he was finally captured by the King's agents. Despite being in custody, however, someone contrived to decapitate him while the ship carrying him back to England was moored in a French port. Isabella could finally rest easy, knowing that her son would never discover her darkest secret!

Karma and the assassin (1407)

Duke Louis of Orléans was assassinated in Paris on 23 November 1407. He was accosted in the street by more than a dozen masked men and stabbed to death. The mastermind behind the assassination was a rival nobleman, Duke John of Burgundy. Normally under such circumstances, the high-ranking instigator of the assassination would keep his mouth shut and let his hired henchmen take the rap. But the Duke of Burgundy was different – they didn't call him John the Fearless for nothing. He made no secret of his role in the assassination and even boasted of it.

You can't escape the inexorable workings of karma, however. Twelve years later, on 10 September 1419, John the Fearless was himself assassinated on the orders of the future King Charles VII of France... who just happened to be a nephew of Duke Louis of Orléans!

The Hashashin assassins (1192)

During the Crusades, the European crusaders were led by a figurehead “King of Jerusalem”. In principle this was a hereditary position, but if the heir was a woman then the title was given to her husband. This was the situation at the time of the Third Crusade, which began in 1189 under the leadership of England’s King Richard the Lionheart. Officially the heir to the crown of Jerusalem was Queen Sibylla, so by convention it was her husband Guy who was recognized as king. Guy was a pathetically weak ruler, but he was a close ally and relative of Richard the Lionheart – who was a strong enough leader in his own right – so the situation suited Richard perfectly.

A problem arose in 1190 when Sibylla died. In Guy’s view, despite the death of his wife, he was still king of Jerusalem. Richard agreed, but others didn’t. Technically Sibylla had been monarch, and on her death the title should have passed to her younger sister, Isabella. A few months after Sibylla died, an ambitious nobleman named Conrad of Montferrat had married Isabella with exactly this prospect in mind. He immediately began to assert his claim to the kingship of Jerusalem.

For over a year there was an intense feud between Guy, supported by Richard the Lionheart, and Conrad, who was supported by many continental noblemen. Eventually, in April 1192, the kingship was put to the vote – and Conrad won.

The reign of King Conrad of Jerusalem was a short one. Within days of his election, he was approached in the street by two men dressed as monks. Suddenly drawing swords from under their cloaks, they hacked Conrad to death. One of the men was killed on the spot by Conrad’s bodyguards, while the other was arrested. It emerged that the killers had been members of a fringe Islamic sect called the Hashashin. Amongst other things, the sect specialized in assassination – in fact the very word “assassin” is derived from Hashashin. The question was – who ordered the assassination of King Conrad?

The Islamic leader at the time was the legendary Saladin – widely considered to be a man of great honour, even by the Europeans he fought against. Saladin had more respect for Conrad than he did for Guy, and he didn't like the Hashashin – so he comes across as a very unlikely suspect in the murder.

The surviving assassin claimed that Richard the Lionheart had ordered the murder. This proves nothing, though. Since Richard was Conrad's best known enemy, the person behind the killing would almost certainly have instructed the assassins to pin the blame on him in the event that they were captured. Despite this, many people did believe in Richard's guilt. While he was making his way back through Europe after the crusade, he was arrested by a former ally of Conrad and charged with his murder. Richard was released after the payment of an enormous ransom, but the shadow of the accusation still hung over him.

The strongest argument against Richard's involvement is the fact that he made no attempt to benefit from the assassination. He didn't try to regain the kingship of Jerusalem for his friend Guy, who by this time was doing very well as Lord of Cyprus. Instead, the new king of Jerusalem was Isabella's new husband, Henry of Champagne, whom she married just a week after Conrad's murder. Anyone looking for the true instigator of that murder need look no further than Henry... at least, not if they subscribe to the *cui bono* school of conspiracy theories!

The mystery of Tutankhamun (1323 BC)

Tutankhamun is often viewed as the greatest of the ancient Egyptian pharaohs. His name is the best known, and his tomb is the most magnificent – opulently decorated and packed to overflowing with gold and other treasures.

Appealing as it is, this picture is almost wholly inaccurate – skewed by the fact that Tutankhamun's tomb was discovered amid great fanfare as recently as 1922. The truth is that he was a relatively minor Pharaoh, whose reign was so insignificant that almost nothing was recorded about it. That's why it took so long to find his tomb, and why – unlike other royal tombs – it had not already been picked clean by grave robbers when it was found. Compared with other Egyptian kings, Tutankhamun's tomb is unusually small – more like that of a court official. The treasure it contained, while extravagant to modern eyes, was decidedly sub-standard for a member of the Egyptian Royal Family.

There's no doubt that Tutankhamun really was a full-fledged Pharaoh, so why was he interred in such a small tomb, and why was there so little record of his decade-long reign? Most historians agree he was the victim of some kind of conspiracy, but after such a vast interval of time it's difficult to make out the details.

Tutankhamun's mummified body was found inside his tomb. It's been subjected to numerous forensic examinations, which show clear indications of physical injuries – including a massive blow to the head sufficient to cause immediate death. Historians are divided as to the cause of this – it might have been murder, or an accident... or murder contrived to look like an accident.

Who benefited from Tutankhamun's death? The most obvious suspect is a senior court official named Ay, who succeeded Tutankhamun as Pharaoh. Because Tutankhamun was so young – eight or nine years old – when he ascended to the throne, Ay ran the country's affairs on his behalf. As the young king approached maturity, however, it began to look like Ay's days in power were numbered. He may have decided to take action to consolidate his position. Tutankhamun was killed when he was barely 18, and his young widow was married by the much older Ay – who became Pharaoh as a result. It was Ay who organized Tutankhamun's funeral... and there is a strong suspicion that he had the boy-king interred in his own tomb, while commandeering Tutankhamun's tomb for himself.

As it turned out, Ay needed his tomb sooner than he would have liked. He died just four years after Tutankhamun, and was succeeded as Pharaoh by the commander-in-chief of the Egyptian army, Horemheb. Unlike his two predecessors, Horemheb had a long reign – almost 30 years. During that time, he made a few changes. It was Horemheb who systematically erased records of Tutankhamun's reign, almost obliterating him from history. He did the same for Ay as well.

So in the long run, Horemheb was the biggest winner. Does that mean he was the real brains behind Tutankhamun's premature death... and Ay's as well?

Conspiracy theories in the ancient world (336 BC)

Alexander the Great is one of the best known figures of ancient Greece. He crushed the powerful Persian Empire, and went on to create an even larger empire of his own. Yet his entire reign was an accident of history. He came to power at the age of 20, when his father – King Philip II of Macedon – was assassinated. If the assassination had never happened, Philip would have been just 58 – and probably still in power – when Alexander died twelve years later.

Philip II was murdered by Pausanias of Orestis, one of his seven bodyguards. Pausanias was immediately killed by the other bodyguards, so he never got the chance to explain why he did what he did. In the centuries following the killing, numerous theories have been put forward – including the obvious one that Pausanias was acting on the orders of Alexander the Great. After all, Alexander was the one who benefited most from the situation. The idea of Alexander's culpability was first proposed by the Roman historian Justin in the 2nd century AD... demonstrating that conspiracy theories are nothing new!

Chapter 4: Hidden agendas

The Glomar Explorer (1974)

Towards the end of June 1974 a huge new ship set out from California into the Pacific Ocean. Called the *Glomar Explorer*, she was longer than two football fields and displaced a massive 56,000 tons. The ship headed straight for a very specific location, about 1700 miles northwest of Hawaii, and hovered over that point – where the water was known to be more than three miles deep. The *Glomar* remained on station for over a month, while the crew lowered a huge, eight-clawed grappling arm all the way to the bottom.

The *Glomar Explorer* was said to be the brainchild of Howard Hughes, a billionaire industrialist famous for undertaking eccentric ventures. Like all his operations, the *Glomar* mission was shrouded in secrecy, but the news filtered out that Hughes was trying to retrieve a valuable deposit of manganese nodules that had been discovered on the ocean floor. The story didn't make a lot of sense, because there are simpler and cheaper ways of obtaining manganese... but people accepted it because Hughes had done equally outrageous things in the past.

There was more to the situation than met the eye, however. Although Hughes had put up some of the money for the *Glomar Explorer*, most of the funding had come from the CIA. It was the CIA, not Hughes, who had commissioned the giant vessel in the first place, and the CIA had supplied her crew. The ship wasn't trying to retrieve manganese nodules from the seabed – it was trying to retrieve a sunken Russian submarine.

The *Golf II* submarine had crashed to the bottom of the Pacific in March 1968. The Soviets had no idea where it was, but the US Navy had a much more effective submarine tracking network. They knew exactly where the wreck of the *Golf* was. The US Navy, however, had no particular interest in retrieving the wreck. The old diesel-powered submarine had been obsolete when it sank, and it had little in common with the latest generation of Soviet nuclear-powered subs. The three nuclear missiles on board the *Golf* were equally obsolete, with only a sixth the range of the latest Russian missiles.

It was true that the wreck of *Golf* might contain some useful information, in the form of code books and cryptographic equipment, but lifting the whole submarine to the surface wasn't the most sensible way to retrieve them. The Navy's scientific advisors informed them that the speed with which the submarine had crashed into the seabed would have left it in a very fragile condition. The chances that it could be brought to the surface intact, through three miles of crushing ocean pressure, was virtually nil.

The CIA, on the other hand, was adamant that the stricken *Golf* had to be brought to the surface. If nothing else, it would demonstrate to the Russians just how superior the United States really was. The US president, Richard Nixon, agreed with the CIA... and the *Glomar Explorer* mission went ahead.

The operation was a disaster. The *Glomar's* giant, octopus-like claw managed to grab hold of the Russian sub and ease it off the seabed... but before it was a third of the way to the surface the whole thing disintegrated. The Navy scientists had been right. When the claw eventually broke surface, all it was holding was the ten metre forward section of the hundred-metre long submarine. No missiles, no code books, no cryptographic equipment... nothing of use to the CIA. Far from demonstrating the superiority of the Americans, they merely succeeded in demonstrating their incompetence.

On August 8 1974, as the *Glomar Explorer* was heading home after its failed mission, the news came in that President Nixon had resigned in the wake of a completely different fiasco – the Watergate scandal.

The H-bomb deception (1957)

The atomic bombs dropped on Hiroshima and Nagasaki in 1945 were the most destructive weapons the world had ever seen. Based on a nuclear fission reaction, they produced an explosive energy that could be measured in kilotons – the equivalent of thousands of tons of conventional explosive.

Almost immediately, scientists realized there was a way to make an even more powerful weapon. The intense heat from the fission reaction could be used to initiate another type of nuclear reaction, fusion, in elements such as hydrogen. The energy produced by such a reaction would be measured not in kilotons but megatons – millions of tons of conventional explosive. The new type of weapon was dubbed an "H-Bomb", standing for hydrogen bomb, to distinguish it from the first generation of atomic bombs which were referred to as A-bombs.

The first successful H-bomb was developed by the Americans in 1952, closely followed by the Russians the following year. Britain was lagging a long way behind. The British government desperately wanted an H-bomb – not so much because they needed it as a weapon, but because of the political bargaining power it would give them. Britain wanted to be a nuclear superpower in the same league as the United States and the Soviet Union.

British scientists had worked alongside the Americans in the development of the original atomic bomb, during the Second World War. At that time the US government was happy to share its nuclear know-how with its transatlantic ally. But in 1946 Congress passed a new Atomic Energy Act, which – amongst other things – vetoed any further collaboration of this type. Britain was on its own.

After frantic efforts to reverse-engineer everything they could learn from the Russian and American tests, Britain announced that it had succeeded in building its own H-bomb. Three tests were carried out at Malden Island, in the middle of the Pacific Ocean, during May and June 1957. All the tests resulted in huge explosions and impressive mushroom clouds. A press release stated that the three tests had involved H-bombs with explosive yields in the megaton range.

This wasn't true. The explosive yields were measured in hundreds of kilotons, not megatons. Whatever the Malden Island tests were, they weren't correctly functioning H-bombs. Two of them may have been H-bombs in which the fusion part of the reaction failed to take place, while at least one of them was simply a very large A-bomb. But those facts weren't known at the time, and it was generally believed that Britain was now a fully fledged member of the exclusive H-bomb club.

As such, the Americans were now happy to share their nuclear secrets with the British – and as a result Britain was able to build H-bombs that really worked. But was this a good thing for Britain, or a bad thing?

It seems inconceivable that the US government was duped to the point of genuinely believing that the British tests had been successful. On the other hand, they may have been as desperate to share their technology with Britain as the British themselves were. The problem was, they couldn't do it openly unless Britain already had an H-bomb capability. If the Americans shared their nuclear secrets with one of their allies, there was no telling who the Russians might choose to share their secrets with.

Britain's reasons for wanting the H-bomb were political – they believed it would give them more power on the international stage. America's motives were equally political – they wanted Britain to feel an enduring sense of obligation to them. It's probably no coincidence that in virtually every major conflict since 1957, Britain has chosen to support the United States!

The Dieppe Raid (1942)

The D-Day landing on the northern coast of France in June 1944 was one of the most carefully planned and executed operations of the Second World War. But it wasn't the first time the Allies had launched a large-scale amphibious assault on that coast. An earlier attempt at landing, on 19 August 1942, was an unmitigated disaster.

The event is usually referred to as the Dieppe "raid", giving the impression that it was a small-scale affair. But that's not the case. No fewer than six thousand troops were put ashore, along a 15-mile stretch of coast centred on the major port of Dieppe. Almost immediately, however, things started to go wrong. The German defences proved too much for the Allies, and the operation was called off after less than six hours. Only half the men who landed made it back to the English coast – the rest were either killed or captured. More than 30 vessels were sunk, including a destroyer, and over a hundred support aircraft were shot down.

The fact that Dieppe had such tragic results tends to overshadow another important issue – why was it undertaken in the first place? Even if it had been successful, what could it possibly have achieved?

In broad terms, there are two reasons for carrying out a beach landing. The most obvious is to establish a beachhead in preparation for a full-scale invasion – as was the case with D-Day two years later. That can't have been the intention at Dieppe, though. The landing force was large enough that it might, in principle, have been able to seize control of the port from the Germans... but there was nothing to back it up. Behind the 6,000 troops who landed, there should have been thousands more waiting to follow them... and there weren't.

At the other extreme there is the commando raid. The intention here is to infiltrate an enemy position, collect intelligence and/or carry out acts of sabotage, and then withdraw. The emphasis is on stealth and covertness – it calls for a small team of highly trained individuals, not an amphibious invasion force. Despite the name historians have given it, the Dieppe raid wasn't a commando operation.

If Dieppe wasn't a full-scale invasion, and it wasn't a commando raid, then what was it? The official line is that it was a massive training exercise, to test Allied operational procedures while at the same time getting a measure of German strengths and weaknesses. The aim was simply to hold the port for a few hours and then withdraw.

This is patent nonsense. In the 3000 years of recorded military history, no-one has ever seen the need to invade a hostile country for a few hours by way of a training exercise. The operation would have been just as beneficial to the enemy as it was to the Allies – it allowed the Germans to test their own operational procedures, while getting a measure of Allied strengths and weaknesses at the same time!

So what about Conspiracy Theories? This is where things start to make sense. In 1942, the bulk of the German army was fighting on the Eastern front, concentrating its efforts on defeating the Soviet Union. The Soviets, in order to relieve pressure on themselves, wanted to see the Germans fighting on a second front in France. On the other hand, the Western allies – Britain and America – much preferred to have the Germans wear themselves out fighting the Russians.

But how could Britain and America convince the Russians that it was impossible to open up a second front in France? The half-hearted Dieppe raid may have been the answer. It may be that it was planned to fail in a more subtle way, with far fewer Allied casualties than actually occurred. Or perhaps, as some Conspiracy Theorists maintain, the casualties were part of the plan all along. It's suspicious, anyway, that most of the victims were neither British or American – they were Canadian.

Regime change in Afghanistan (1839)

During the 19th century, the independent nation of Afghanistan was effectively a buffer state between the Russian Empire and India, which was part of the British Empire at the time. In the early years of the century, Afghanistan was ruled by the Durrani dynasty – which was fine with the British government, because most of the Durranis were favourably disposed towards them.

Then in 1823 the Durranis were deposed by a new ruler, Dost Mohammad Khan. Dost Mohammad had no particular axe to grind against the British, but as time went on he realized there was more to gain by cultivating ties with the Russians instead. This was a disastrous development as far as Britain was concerned.

One solution to the problem would have been to invade Afghanistan, take it over by force, and annex it to the British Empire. In the late 1830s, when the crisis arose, there was no doubt that Britain had the military capability to achieve this. But the approach had its drawbacks. It would aggravate the Russians, and might have led to war with Russia – which was the last thing Britain wanted.

It would be simpler if Dost Mohammad could be deposed in favour of one of his predecessors, Shah Shuja Durrani, who still had a claim to the throne and would be much more accommodating to British interests. On 1 October 1838 the British Governor General of India, Lord Auckland, issued the Simla Manifesto, announcing Britain's intention to support Shah Shuja's claim to the Afghan throne – using whatever force was necessary.

Two months later, in December 1838, a huge Anglo-Indian army set off on a northward march into Afghanistan. By August of the following year the British had taken Kabul. Dost Mohammad was forced to flee the city, leaving Shah Shuja to be reinstated as the legitimate ruler of Afghanistan... or, for those of a more cynical frame of mind, as Britain's puppet leader.

Having achieved what they set out to do, most of the troops returned to India, leaving just a small garrison in Kabul. From a British point of view, the whole Afghan problem had been settled in a highly satisfactory way – what could possibly go wrong now?

As it turned out, there was one small detail the British planners had overlooked. The Afghans didn't want Shah Shuja running the country – they wanted Dost Mohammad. The Kabul garrison found itself on the receiving end of rebel attacks led by Dost Mohammad's son, Akbar Khan. The British envoy to Kabul, Sir William Macnaghten, was forced to open negotiations with Akbar. But the talks didn't go well. Following a particularly heated exchange in December 1841, Akbar placed his pistol in Macnaghten's mouth and pulled the trigger. Three of Macnaghten's aides were killed at the same meeting.

The following month, the British decided it was time to withdraw from Kabul. Something like 4,000 troops and 12,000 civilians began the slow march back to India – but only a handful of them made it. The rest were killed in an ambush about 50 miles south-east of Kabul. Less than three months later, on 5 April 1842, Shah Shuja was assassinated... and Dost Mohammad Khan was restored to the Afghan throne.

Soviet war machines, British technology (1946)

The MiG-15 was the first really successful jet fighter, fielded in huge numbers by the Soviet Union and its allies during the late 1940s and early 50s. The plane's success was down to its combination of a first-class airframe, designed by the Mikoyan-Gurevich Bureau of Moscow, and a first-class engine, designed by the Rolls-Royce company of Derby, England.

When the Second World War ended in 1945, the Russians were lagging a long way behind Britain and America in jet technology. The following year the British Prime Minister, Clement Attlee, presented the Soviet Union with a fully functional Rolls-Royce Nene turbojet, complete with permission to produce it under licence, by way of thanks for the support the Soviets had given to Britain during the War.

In light of the subsequent polarization of the Cold War – which saw America and Britain on one side and Russia on the other – Attlee's behaviour may appear to border on treason. But that wasn't the case at the time. The Russians had been wartime allies of Britain just as much as the Americans had, and in political terms Attlee's Labour Party was poised midway between Soviet-style communism and American-style capitalism. That was little consolation four years later, however, when British pilots found themselves up against the MiG-15 in the Korean War!

Pride's Purge (1648)

The English Civil War was all about power. It began, in 1642, as a straightforward power struggle between King Charles I and Parliament. Most Parliamentarians had no particular desire to oust the King – they simply wanted him to concede a greater share of power to Parliament. What they were looking for, in short, was democracy.

As the war progressed, Parliament gradually gained the upper hand. It did so for one very good reason – because its army was superior to that of the Royalists. In 1645, the Parliamentarian forces were reorganized into the New Model Army – the first truly professional army the country had ever seen. Its generals – men like Thomas Fairfax and Oliver Cromwell – were supremely competent... and supremely ambitious. They may have been fighting for Parliament, but that didn't mean they agreed with its democratic agenda.

When Charles I was captured in 1647, Parliament embarked on a series of negotiations with him. But the King stalled for time, stringing the talks out without making any real concessions. While the politicians saw this as business as usual, the leaders of the New Model Army were infuriated. In November 1648, Fairfax issued a remonstrance calling for an end to negotiations – and for the King to be put on trial as an enemy of the state.

To Fairfax's disgust, Parliament rejected his remonstrance by 125 votes to 58. That meant there were no fewer than 125 traitors in the House of Commons! Or if they weren't exactly traitors, then at least they were political moderates... which in the Army's eyes was almost as bad.

The time for talk was over – what Fairfax needed now was action. He called in one of his Colonels, a man named Thomas Pride, together with the infantry regiment he commanded. Pride's regiment was going to go down in history – as the instigators of the only successful military takeover Britain has ever seen.

On 6 December 1648, Pride's men took up their places outside the House of Commons. Pride himself stood at the top of the steps with a list in his hand. As the members of Parliament arrived, he checked their names against the list. If they were on it he let them through into the chamber. If their names weren't on the list they were taken away and locked up.

By the end of Pride's Purge, there were only about 70 members of Parliament left. By a strange coincidence, all of them concurred with the Army's view that further negotiations with the King were pointless. On 4 January 1649 the Rump Parliament, as it became known, voted to put Charles I on trial for treason.

The trial didn't take long. It began on 20 January and ended a week later with a guilty verdict. The King was sentenced to death, and beheaded on 30 January. With the monarchy abolished and Parliament purged, England was effectively controlled by the Army... and would remain so until the restoration of Charles II in 1660.

Machiavelli (1513)

Scheming and duplicitous politicians are often referred to as Machiavellian. The word comes from Niccolò Machiavelli, who lived in Renaissance Florence at the same time as Leonardo da Vinci. Machiavelli spent some time working as a politician, although there's no evidence he was an especially Machiavellian one. His notoriety rests not on his political career but on a book called *The Prince* that he wrote in 1513. Addressed to a young Prince, the book is packed full of cynical advice for the aspiring politician. No-one is quite sure whether Machiavelli intended this advice to be taken seriously, or if it's meant as a tongue-in-cheek political satire.

The most famous passage in *The Prince* comes from Chapter 18: "In the actions of all men, and especially of princes, one looks to the end... The means will be judged honorable and praised by everyone, because the masses are always taken in by appearances and with the outcome of the thing." As with much of Machiavelli's writing, this is unnecessarily wordy – it is usually paraphrased in much simpler terms: The end justifies the means.

Murder of Thomas Becket, Archbishop of Canterbury

Murder in the cathedral (1170)

During the Middle Ages, senior figures in the church hierarchy had enormous power. So much power, in fact, that they were effectively political positions rather than religious ones – certainly too important to be entrusted to a mere priest.

In 1162, King Henry II of England needed to choose a new Archbishop of Canterbury. At the time, this was the most senior church position in the country – as it still is, of course. But in those days, when the church had far more influence on worldly affairs than it does today, the Archbishop of Canterbury was a position that had real power.

Henry decided to give the role to a close friend and ally of his called Thomas Becket. He needed someone who would support him politically, while being astute enough to deal with matters of state – and Becket struck him as ideal. He already held the position of Lord Chancellor, and making him Archbishop of Canterbury was the obvious next step.

There was one problem – it may be a minor technicality, but an Archbishop has to be a priest. Becket wasn't – he was a politician. This wasn't a huge obstacle, though, and Becket was fast-tracked through the process. He was ordained as a priest on 2 June 1162, and installed as Archbishop of Canterbury the following day – 3 June 1162.

Unfortunately for Henry II, Becket took his new job seriously. In conflicts between the church and the state, Becket stood up for the church. Before long, he became the biggest thorn in the King's side.

There is a well-known story that Henry uttered something along the lines of "Who will rid me of this turbulent priest?", which was interpreted by a group of four knights as a command to assassinate the Archbishop. The story may or may not be true – but what certainly is true is that Becket ended up hacked to death by the four knights in his own cathedral.

In the immediate aftermath of the murder, Becket's demise was seen as a tragedy. Whether or not the King had been responsible for it, his reputation suffered a blow from which it never recovered. Becket himself was hailed as a martyr to the church, and a cult soon grew up around the veneration of his relics.

During his lifetime, however, Becket had never been a popular figure – being seen as a politician in priest's clothing. This view has emerged again in recent times – a BBC poll in 2006 voted him the second worst figure in British history after Jack the Ripper. Why? Because, as the BBC website gleefully pointed out, Becket was the "founder of gesture politics and master of the soundbite"!

Massacre on St. Brice's Day (1002)

Ethelred the Unready was one of the last Saxon kings of England. He came to power at the tender age of ten, when his older brother Edward was assassinated in 978. It's unlikely that young Ethelred had a hand in the assassination, although it was almost certainly the work of people who wanted to see him on the throne.

Ethelred went on to gain a dubious distinction – he's the only English king in history who is universally known by an insulting epithet. Unready means "ill-advised" in Anglo-Saxon, not "unprepared" as a modern reader might suppose – but it's still a pejorative. Whether he was ill-advised or unprepared, Ethelred was a lousy monarch.

King Ethelred had a problem with Danes. These weren't marauding, horn-helmeted Vikings who raided England's shores, but a more subtle kind of invader – Danish immigrants. Ethelred didn't like immigrants – he thought they were plotting to overthrow him and take over the country. He tried various measures, but nothing worked. Then in November 1002 he had a brainwave.

Ethelred's solution to the Danish problem was the same as Adolf Hitler's solution to the Jewish problem. He was going to exterminate all of them. Ethelred dispatched secret letters to the various cities of his kingdom instructing that on a certain day – 13 November 1002, the feast-day of Saint Brice – all persons of Danish extraction should be seized and put to death. It's not known how widely the order was carried out, but there's no doubt the massacre took place in at least some cities. One of them was Oxford, where the bodies of dozens of victims were unearthed in 2008.

Two years after the massacre, in 1004, Ethelred was still boasting about how "a decree was sent out by me with the counsel of my leading men and magnates, to the effect that all the Danes who had sprung up in this island, sprouting like cockle amongst the wheat, were to be destroyed by a most just extermination."

Unfortunately for Ethelred, St Brice's Day didn't put an end to the Danish threat. The Danes may or may not have been plotting to take over England before the massacre, but they certainly were after it. One of the victims was the sister of the Danish king, Sweyn Forkbeard, and that made it personal. By 1013 Ethelred had been ousted, and England had a new king – Sweyn Forkbeard. Although Ethelred and the Saxons fought back, they were on the back foot now. The St Brice's Day Massacre was the beginning of the end for Saxon England.

Another cathedral, another murder (1079)

History repeats itself. Almost a century before Thomas Becket was assassinated in Canterbury Cathedral, something very similar happened a thousand miles away in southern Poland. The victim on this occasion was Stanislaus of Szczepanów, who was the Archbishop of Kraków – a post held nine centuries later by Karol Wojtyła, who went on to become Pope John Paul II.

Like Karol Wojtyła, Stanislaus of Szczepanów found himself in conflict with the government of his time. In Wojtyła's case it was the Communists – with Stanislaus it was King Bolesław the Bold. Being bold, the King didn't waste time dropping subtle hints the way Henry II did a hundred years later. He went straight to Kraków Cathedral and dealt with the matter personally. He slew the archbishop as he was celebrating mass, and hacked his body into pieces.

As with Becket, the murder didn't prove as universally popular as Bolesław might have hoped. He was ousted from power later the same year, and forced to flee the country... while Stanislaus was made a saint.

Chapter 5: Convenient deaths

The strange death of General Sikorski (1943)

After the German invasion of Poland in 1939, a Polish government-in-exile was set up in London. This was led by General Władysław Sikorski, who acted both as Prime Minister of the exiled government and as Commander-in-Chief of the Polish armed forces. Sikorski was a forceful and committed leader, who stood up for Polish interests even when they conflicted with those of his British hosts.

When the bodies of 20,000 Polish officers were found massacred in Katyn Forest in April 1943, the immediate reaction of the British government was to blame the atrocity on the Nazis – after all, they were the enemy. But Sikorski rocked the boat by suggesting that the perpetrators were not the Germans but the Russians – Britain's most powerful political allies after the Americans. For General Sikorski, this was like biting the hand that fed him. If the British had been suspicious of him before, they were even more suspicious now.

On 24 May 1943, Sikorski embarked on a tour of Polish troops stationed in Palestine and the Lebanon. He travelled with his entourage in a converted Liberator bomber, registration number AL523, piloted by a Czech Flight Lieutenant named Prchal. The first leg of the journey took them from RAF Lyneham in Wiltshire to the British base on Gibraltar. The next day they left Gibraltar on the second leg, heading for Cairo.

While the Liberator was in the air, a curious incident took place in London. The Polish Minister of Works received a phone call from an anonymous man speaking in good Polish, who gave him a brief and startling message before hanging up: "General

Sikorski's plane has crashed at Gibraltar, and all its passengers have been killed." Alarmed, the Minister phoned two colleagues – the Deputy Prime Minister and the Deputy Defence Minister – and discovered they had received almost identical messages. But after further frantic phone calls, it became clear the whole thing was a hoax – nothing untoward had occurred at Gibraltar, and General Sikorski's plane had landed safely in Cairo.

Sikorski's tour of the Middle East lasted six weeks, ending as it had begun in Cairo. On 3 July a transport aircraft arrived to take him back to England. It was Liberator AL523, once again piloted by Flight Lieutenant Prchal. The first leg of the return journey, taking them back to Gibraltar, passed without incident. But 16 seconds after lifting off from Gibraltar, the Liberator crashed into the sea. Everyone on board was killed except Prchal. The exact conditions of the hoax telephone call had been fulfilled, six weeks after it had been made: "General Sikorski's plane has crashed at Gibraltar, and all its passengers have been killed."

The cause of the crash remains a mystery. The official enquiry found no evidence of sabotage or pilot error, and placed the blame on an unspecified mechanical failure. Others have speculated that the crash was caused by the unusual loading of the plane, or by freak weather conditions, or by a bizarre accident involving a loose mailbag that fell through the nose wheel doors during take-off.

And then there are the conspiracy theories. The Liberator may have been sabotaged by Nazi agents, who had an active cell on Gibraltar at the time. Prchal may have been bribed to crash the plane... his testimony contains odd inconsistencies. Sikorski may have been assassinated by the Russians – or even the British – because he was asking awkward questions about the Katyn massacre.

The strangest thing about the case, however, is the phone call – made six weeks before the crash, yet uncannily accurate in its details. It may have been sheer coincidence, of course – a hoax that just happened to foreshadow real events. On the other hand, it might indicate that there really was a plot to kill Sikorski at Gibraltar, and the informant simply got the date wrong.

Rasputin (1916)

In the last years of the Russian Empire, Grigori Rasputin was the most influential advisor to Tsar Nicholas II and his family. In the eyes of many, Rasputin was the real power behind the Empire, with the Tsar simply doing whatever Rasputin told him to. It's not surprising, therefore, that some people were unhappy with the extent of Rasputin's influence. In December 1916, Rasputin was assassinated.

There's no doubt that Rasputin was the victim of a conspiracy – the question is, how far did the conspiracy go? The murder took place at the palace of Prince Felix Yusupov in Saint Petersburg, and the most prominent instigators of the conspiracy were Yusupov himself and a group of his close associates. But were there other, more powerful, figures lurking in the shadows?

Prince Yusupov's own account of the murder was outrageously gothic, with Rasputin portrayed as being supernaturally difficult to kill, while Yusupov himself played a kind of heroic vampire-hunter role. According to the Prince, Rasputin was first poisoned with cyanide, then shot several times. There was no visible effect – Rasputin fought off his attackers and managed to escape from the palace. Outside he was shot again, then beaten with a club, and finally dumped into an icy river.

Rasputin (1916)

At least parts of Yusupov's account are borne out by the evidence. Two days after the murder, Rasputin's body was fished out of the river. An autopsy revealed no trace of cyanide in his body, but he had been shot several times and severely beaten up. Most of the physical injuries, however, appeared to have been inflicted after death – which was caused by a bullet through the forehead.

Significantly, the fatal bullet appeared to have been fired by a different gun than the other bullets that hit Rasputin. This conflicts with Yusupov's testimony, in which he was the only person to have fired any shots. Yet the fatal bullet didn't come from a Russian gun. Judging by the wound it inflicted, it was a non-jacketed round of the type which, at the time, was only used in one type of weapon – the British Webley revolver.

As far as anyone can determine, there was only one Webley revolver in Saint Petersburg in December 1916. It belonged to a member of the British Secret Service named Oswald Rayner – who just happened to be an old friend of Felix Yusupov. They had studied at Oxford University together, and Rayner was a frequent visitor to Yusupov's palace... he was known to have been there on the day of the murder, in fact. The connection between Rayner and Yusupov was noted by none other than Tsar Nicholas himself, who complained to the British Ambassador about it. But two months later the Tsar was deposed, and whatever interest there had been in pursuing those responsible for Rasputin's murder evaporated.

An obvious question arises out of all of this – what possible reason could Britain have for assassinating a Russian political advisor? There was a very good reason, as it turns out. In 1916 – the height of the First World War – Britain was locked in a deadly conflict with Germany. Russia was also fighting Germany, but on the Eastern rather than the Western Front. Rasputin was urging the Tsar to call a ceasefire on the Eastern Front – which would have freed up yet more German troops for the Western Front. That wasn't something Britain was in any hurry to see.

Émile Zola and the Dreyfus Affair (1902)

In September 1894 French military intelligence uncovered an act of espionage – someone in the French Army was handing over secrets to the Germans. Suspicion soon fell on a junior artillery officer named Alfred Dreyfus, largely because Dreyfus was the only person of Jewish extraction who could possibly have committed the crime. Anti-Semitism was endemic in the French military at the time. There was no substantive evidence against Dreyfus – for the very good reason that he was completely innocent – but he was the perfect scapegoat. He was convicted in December 1894 and sentenced to life imprisonment.

Dreyfus was deported to Devil's Island off the coast of South America. The island was essentially a one-man prison – its only inhabitants were Dreyfus and his guards. As far as the French authorities were concerned, the incarceration of Dreyfus should have been the end of the affair. In fact, it was only the beginning.

In April 1896 a new man, Georges Picquart, was appointed head of French military intelligence. While reading himself into the new post, Picquart discovered an astonishing fact. There was clear evidence showing that the spy was not Alfred Dreyfus but another officer named Ferdinand Esterhazy. When Picquart showed the evidence to his superiors, they fabricated counter-evidence that reinforced the case against Dreyfus. Picquart's evidence was hushed up, and Esterhazy was publicly cleared of any involvement. Picquart himself was reposted to North Africa.

If the Dreyfus affair is France's Watergate, then Émile Zola was its Woodward and Bernstein. Zola, one of the best known writers in France at the time, blew the lid off the conspiracy in dramatic fashion. On 13 January 1898, he published a front-page newspaper article entitled *J'accuse* – in which he did just that. He accused Esterhazy of being the real spy, and he accused the French authorities of deliberately concealing the fact. He accused them of falsely convicting Dreyfus, and of fabricating all the evidence against him. And Zola named names.

Émile Zola's article polarized France. Some people saw the author as a hero, fighting for truth and justice, while others saw him as a traitor – an enemy of France. Everyone had an opinion on the subject, and usually it was a strong one. Zola received numerous death threats, and several attempts were made to assassinate him. One of them may have been successful.

Zola's death certificate, dated 29 September 1902, states that he died of carbon monoxide poisoning. The immediate cause of the gas build-up was a blocked chimney. But chimneys don't just block themselves – not when the victim is the most controversial figure in Paris, anyway. It was too late to silence Zola – he had said enough already – but revenge was another matter. There was no shortage of anti-Dreyfus activists who wanted to punish Zola for his support of the person they imagined to be an enemy of the state.

The Dreyfus scandal bubbled on for several more years, but eventually the truth won out. Alfred Dreyfus was formally cleared of all charges against him in 1906, four years after Émile Zola's death. But there were still people who couldn't accept the truth. In 1908, while Zola's ashes were being interred at the Pantheon in Paris, Dreyfus was shot by a would-be assassin. Fortunately the attempt was unsuccessful, and Dreyfus lived on for another 27 years.

Who killed Napoleon? (1821)

The first 15 years of the 19th century were dominated by Napoleon Bonaparte. A large part of continental Europe was absorbed into Napoleon's French Empire, while other countries – Britain included – were forced to throw all their resources into the Napoleonic Wars. Finally, in 1815, Napoleon was defeated at the Battle of Waterloo. After surrendering to the British he was taken to the remote island of Saint Helena in the South Atlantic.

The idea was to make sure that Napoleon couldn't cause any more trouble. He had been exiled once before, on the island of Elba in the Mediterranean, but he had escaped after just ten months. He wasn't going to escape again if his captors had their way. He still had plenty of supporters who wanted to see him rise again, but they were a long way from Saint Helena.

Napoleon was placed in the custody of the Governor of Saint Helena – a nasty piece of work named Sir Hudson Lowe. He had the former Emperor consigned to a damp and decrepit old building called Longwood House, where the living conditions were appalling. When news of this seeped back to Britain, it caused an upsurge of popular support for the country's erstwhile arch-enemy, while Lowe was portrayed as a kind of pantomime villain. Lowe responded by becoming even nastier – he cut off Napoleon's supply of firewood, forcing him to burn the furniture to keep warm.

People began to suspect that Lowe wanted Napoleon to catch a fatal illness, and was doing everything in his power to hasten that event. The Governor of Saint Helena certainly had good reason to want the former Emperor dead. There were rumours that Napoleon's supporters in the United States – an enemy of Britain at the time – were planning a rescue attempt. If that happened, and if it was successful, it would be the end of Lowe's career. On the other hand, if Napoleon were to die a premature death... that would be much more convenient.

The doctor who had been assigned to Napoleon, Barry O'Meara, was worried about the former Emperor's health – and the conditions he was being kept in. He wrote numerous letters to the British authorities hinting that Lowe was trying to do away with his captive, but all to no avail. Napoleon finally died on 5 May 1821. An autopsy identified the cause of death as a perforated stomach ulcer, which was attributed to cancer. There was no real evidence for this, however. The ulcer could have been caused in many other ways – but since these would have indicated mistreatment on the part of Napoleon's captors, they were quietly ignored.

In thc 1950s, Napoleon's medical records were re-examined with the benefit of more advanced diagnostic knowledge. An astonishing fact emerged – all his symptoms were consistent with arsenic poisoning. Arsenic was a favourite poison in the 19th century, because it's very difficult to detect if administered in small doses over a long period of time. Modern analysis techniques were applied to preserved samples of Napoleon's hair, which were found to contain large quantities of the poison.

So was Napoleon poisoned with arsenic, and was Hudson

Lowe the perpetrator? Lowe certainly did everything he could to hasten his captive's death, so he might well have tried arsenic on top of everything else. Whether he did or not, there seems little doubt that Napoleon would have lived a longer life if he had never met Sir Hudson Lowe.

Character assassination (1762)

Catherine the Great was one of the most powerful female leaders in history, ruling over the Russian Empire for more than 30 years in the second half of the 18th century. But she didn't inherit the throne – her husband did. This was Peter III, who reigned for just six months from January to June 1762. On 28 June, Catherine ousted him from power and had him imprisoned. A week later it was announced that the deposed Emperor had died, although the cause of his death was unspecified.

Did Catherine the Great have her husband assassinated? Probably – he was an obstacle standing in the way of her ambitions. But she needed to go further than that – she had to justify her overthrow of Peter if she was to gain the sympathy of the Russian public.

Based on evidence from his own lifetime, Peter III was an enlightened and intelligent ruler who genuinely cared about his subjects. But that didn't suit Catherine's purpose at all, so she embarked on a systematic programme of character assassination. Peter was portrayed as cruel, stupid, ugly and perverted – a view that persisted into the 20th century before the truth was finally uncovered.

The death that changed history (1612)

Prince Henry Frederick, the eldest son of King James VI of Scotland, was born in 1594. Eleven years later, Henry's father gained a new and even more prestigious title – King James I of England. The young Prince was now heir to the English throne as well as the Scottish one. He took his role seriously, adapting to English court life much more easily than his father. He grew into a popular and athletic teenager who excelled at outdoor activities – unlike his frail and introverted younger brother Charles.

At the age of 16 Henry was given the title of Prince of Wales, and allowed to set up his own court at St James's Palace. This quickly became more popular than the King's own court, much to James's dismay. He's alleged to have said of the ambitious youngster "Will he bury me alive?" Henry certainly had no qualms about crossing his father when he had to. The Prince was a good friend of Sir Walter Raleigh, whom James had imprisoned in the Tower of London. Henry didn't hide the fact that he thought this was the action of a fool.

Prince Henry never lived to become King Henry the Ninth. In the latter part of 1612, when he was still only 18, he developed a serious illness. He ignored it for as long as he could, continuing to play tennis and go about his duties at court. But by the end of October he was confined to bed, and he died on 6 November.

The cause of death was described as "fever" – but this is a symptom and not a cause. People at the time were mystified by the sudden death of such an apparently fit and healthy young man. The fact that the victim was the enormously popular son of a not especially popular king – in a court filled with not especially popular people – only heightened the mystery. Most people assumed it was a simple case of murder – that the Prince of Wales had been poisoned.

But if so, who was behind it? The obvious beneficiary was his younger brother Charles, who became heir to the throne in his place – but Charles was still a few days short of his 12th birthday, so he can't be taken seriously as a suspect. Many people pointed the finger at Henry's father, James I, who made little secret of his jealousy of the Prince. But that doesn't really make sense, because James needed a strong heir. Henry, whatever the King thought of him personally, was the best person for the job.

Another suspect was the King's close advisor Robert Carr. We met him in Chapter 3 – he was involved in the poisoning of Thomas Overbury a year after the death of the Prince of Wales. It's known that Carr and the Prince detested each other, so the theory has its attractions. On the other hand, the consensus among modern historians is that Henry's symptoms indicate a perfectly natural cause of death – Typhoid fever.

Whatever – or whoever – caused the death of Henry Frederick, there can be no doubt it altered the course of history. When James I died in 1625, he was succeeded by Henry's younger brother Charles – who became, as Charles I, one of the least popular kings England has ever had. Parliament declared war on him, and then had him executed for treason. It's difficult to imagine the same thing would have happened to Henry, if he'd lived that long – in fact, there's no telling how English history might have turned out.

Elizabethan drama (1593)

Christopher Marlowe was born just two months before William Shakespeare, and when he grew up he chose the same career – he became a playwright. Marlowe's most famous work is *Doctor Faustus*, about an occultist who makes a pact with the Devil. He also wrote a play about Edward II, who – as we saw in Chapter 3 – was murdered in Berkeley Castle. Before the play could be performed, however, Marlowe himself was murdered.

Marlowe was just 29 years old when he was killed. It happened in South London after a long drinking session in the company of three other men – Robert Poley, Nicholas Skeres and Ingram Frizer. According to the three survivors there was a row about the bill, during which Marlowe attacked Frizer with a knife. Frizer then killed Marlowe in self-defence.

The official inquest into Marlowe's death accepted the account of the three witnesses as being the truth, the whole truth and nothing but the truth. The court agreed the killing was a legitimate act of self-defence, and Frizer was cleared of any responsibility. Even such a mainstream source as the *Daily Telegraph*, however, pointed out in 2012 that "Most scholars believe the inquest, conducted by the Queen's Coroner William Danby, was a cover-up."

The main support for Frizer's story came from Robert Poley and Nicholas Skeres. They weren't just anybody – they were two of the government agents who had infiltrated the Babington Plot six years earlier. As described in Chapter 2, this was a "false flag" operation designed to incriminate Mary Queen of Scots and hasten her execution. If Poley and Skeres had happily conspired in the downfall of a Queen, they were perfectly capable of conspiring in the downfall of a mere playwright.

But why should government agents – or anyone else – want Christopher Marlowe dead? Over the years, at least a dozen different theories have been put forward. A recurring theme is that Marlowe may have been a spy himself – one that knew too much and had to be silenced. There seems little doubt that he led a secretive double life of some kind. He would disappear for extended periods of time, possibly overseas, and reappear with more money than he should have had.

There are other reasons for supposing that Marlowe had enemies in high places. As a writer, he was in an excellent position to cause trouble. His plays are full of subversive ideas – both political, as in *Edward II*, and religious, as in *Doctor Faustus*. There were persistent rumours that Marlowe was a militant atheist, or a secret Catholic. At the time of his death there was a warrant out for his arrest – the authorities had discovered evidence hinting at his involvement in an anti-Protestant movement. Whether this evidence was genuine, or whether it had been fabricated to incriminate Marlowe, no-one really knows.

Another theory holds that Marlowe faked his own death, and that Frizer and the others were covering for him. The young playwright had a good enough reason for wanting to drop out of sight. If the charges against him had been proved, he would have faced a death sentence. But if Marlowe didn't really die, what did he do for the rest of his life? Some people believe he went into the ghost-writing business – his chief client being a second-rate colleague of his named William Shakespeare!

Deposed, imprisoned and dead (1471)

When Henry VI came to the throne in 1422 he was less than a year old. Obviously at that time he was just a figurehead, and the country was run by the people around him. But the situation didn't change as Henry grew up – he remained a puppet throughout his life. In 1461 he was ousted by another claimant to the throne, who was duly crowned as King Edward IV. Less than ten years later, though, the tables were turned – Edward was overthrown by Henry's supporters. Henry VI was back... but not for long.

In the Spring of 1471, Edward IV regained the throne. Henry was imprisoned in the Tower of London... where he was found dead on 22 May. Did Edward have him murdered? The death of his rival was suspiciously well timed, anyway. Henry left no powerful heirs to challenge Edward for the crown, his only son having been killed in battle a few weeks earlier. Indeed, the official line was that Henry died of grief on hearing of his son's death – but few people believed that.

Not everyone blamed King Edward, though. In the third and last of the plays that Shakespeare wrote about Henry VI, he has him stabbed to death by Edward's younger brother – none other than the Bard's favourite villain, the future Richard III.

The sinking of the White Ship (1120)

Henry I was the youngest son of William the Conqueror, and England's third Norman king. It's a modern-day misconception to imagine that the Normans were Frenchmen – in fact they were Vikings, and the French were their mortal enemies. In November

The sinking of the White Ship (1120)

1120 King Henry was on the other side of the Channel, where he had just put the king of France in his place with a series of military victories. At Henry's side was his 17-year old son William, who had been groomed since birth to be his heir.

Henry and his entourage of Norman knights headed home to England. When they arrived at the port of Barfleur on 25 November, the King was approached by a man named Thomas FitzStephen, whose father had been captain of the ship on which Henry's own father had sailed to England in 1066. FitzStephen had a ship of his own, the White Ship, which he claimed was the fastest and most modern in existence. It was agreed that FitzStephen would take

Prince William and the younger knights back to England, while the King and the other senior nobles travelled ahead of them in another ship.

As soon as the more mature members of the party had left the scene, however, the youngsters started drinking. By the time they were ready to depart, everyone was rolling drunk – including Captain FitzStephen and his crew. Prince William – who was as drunk as the rest – urged the captain to try and make it back to England before the King's ship did. FitzStephen ordered his men to row as hard as they could. In the dark, off the treacherous coast of Normandy, that was a mistake. The White Ship hit a rock and began to sink.

By sunrise the next day, virtually everyone who had set sail in the White Ship had drowned. The victims included no fewer than 140 knights and eighteen noblewomen – the rich young heirs to many of the greatest estates of England and Normandy. But ultimately only one of the fatalities really mattered – Prince William, the heir to the English throne.

The official view was that the sinking of the White Ship, like the death of Princess Diana almost nine centuries later, was an accident caused by drunkenness. Urged on by his rowdy young passengers, Captain FitzStephen left Barfleur at a speed that was too high for the conditions, and with a reckless disregard for potential hazards. Under the circumstances, an accident wasn't just a possibility – it was virtually inevitable.

Accident or not, there's no doubt the sinking changed the course of history. Some people lost out, while others gained. Few historians seriously believe the White Ship was deliberately sabotaged, but for those who do there is no shortage of potential suspects.

Who benefited from Prince William's death? The most obvious answer is his sister, Matilda, who was next in line to the throne. But Matilda was never crowned – the Norman noblemen hated her because she married a Frenchman. Instead, when King Henry died in 1135, they offered the crown to Matilda's cousin Stephen. The result was almost 20 years of anarchy, during which England was never quite sure if it was ruled by Matilda or Stephen.

So how does Stephen measure up as a suspect? The circumstances look suspicious, to say the least. He was one of the young passengers due to travel on the White Ship, but he never made it on board. He claimed that all the pre-launch drinking had given him diarrhoea, and so he stayed ashore.

Arguably the real winners, however, were the powerful Norman landowners who used the Anarchy – the civil war between Stephen and Matilda – as an excuse to jostle for power and territory among themselves. Taking all of them into account, there are plenty of suspects to choose from!

A hunting accident... allegedly (1100)

William the Conqueror held two titles – Duke of Normandy and King of England. When he died in 1087, his eldest son Robert succeeded him as Duke of Normandy while his third son became King William II of England. The second son, Richard, was already dead – killed 12 years earlier in a hunting accident in the New Forest. William's fourth and final son, Henry, got nothing.

The reign of William II was cut short by another hunting "accident" in the New Forest. He was killed by an arrow fired by a nobleman named Walter Tirel. But was it really an accident? It was described as such at the time, although the circumstances are very suspicious. The King was left alone with Tirel, with no bodyguards, and Tirel fled the country before he could be questioned. William's younger brother Henry – the one who had been left with nothing by his father – also happened to be on the hunting party that day... and he was quick to take advantage of the situation. He was crowned King Henry I of England just three days after his brother's death.

Death of William Rufus

Chapter 6:
Secret identities

The body on Somerton beach (1948)

On the evening of 30 November 1948 an unidentified man was seen on Somerton Beach in South Australia, behaving as if he was drunk. The next morning his dead body was discovered in the same spot. The man hadn't been drunk – he'd been writhing in agony. An autopsy revealed extensive internal damage consistent with poisoning, although no trace of the poison itself was discovered. The authorities jumped to the conclusion that it was suicide – although it's not clear why a suicide should choose a painful, slow-acting poison simply because it was undetectable after death. That looks more like the action of a murderer.

There is other evidence pointing to murder. Why would a suicide take such trouble to remove all evidence of identity? The victim was carrying a few commonplace items, but no wallet or keys that could help to identify him. All the labels had been carefully cut out of his clothes, which were of high quality, and in good condition – this wasn't some homeless down-and-out. There was, however, one very unusual item found on his person. In the fob pocket of his trousers there was a small, tightly rolled scrap of paper bearing the mysterious words "Tamám Shud" in a strange oriental style font.

Tamám Shud is an old Persian phrase roughly corresponding to "The End" in English. It's the closing line of *The Rubaiyat of Omar Khayyam*, by the Victorian poet Edward Fitzgerald. The *Rubaiyat* used to be enormously popular, and at the time of the Somerton case there were thousands of copies floating around the English-speaking world, in dozens of different editions. The copy from which the slip of paper had been torn was found by a local man, dumped in the back of his car a short distance from where the body was discovered. Despite the numerous editions of the book in existence, this one appeared to be unique. Something similar had been produced by a New Zealand publisher, but it wasn't quite the same. The Somerton Man's copy appeared to be one of a kind.

The book was unusual in another way, too. On the inside rear cover, so faint that it could only be read in ultraviolet light, there was a coded message – five lines of handwritten letters with no obvious meaning. The existence of the secret code immediately suggests espionage – as does the apparent uniqueness of the book. This is indicative of a type of encryption system called a one-time pad, which was often used by military intelligence at the time. There would have been just one other copy of the book in existence – held by the person for whom the coded message was intended.

To this day, the body on Somerton beach has never been identified. A telephone number pencilled inside the book gave police a lead to a young local woman, but – like the man who found the book dumped in his car – she was never subjected to rigorous questioning. The same was true of another man she claimed to have given a copy of the *Rubaiyat* to. It was as if the authorities didn't really want to solve the case – again, for conspiracy theorists, a clear indication that military intelligence was involved. If so, there is no shortage of possibilities – at the time of the incident, in 1948, the world was just embarking on a globe-spanning Cold War

.

Jack the Ripper (1888)

Jack the Ripper has a good claim to being the most notorious criminal in history. Five women were murdered in the Whitechapel area of London, in the most brutal way imaginable, in the space of a few months in 1888. The case attracted huge public interest at the time, yet the perpetrator was never caught. The police had numerous suspects, but there was never enough evidence to convict any of them.

How can such a high profile murder go unsolved? One possible answer is that the murderer was a high profile individual himself, and there was a top-level conspiracy to cover up for him. Over the years, numerous names have been put forward, but the most prestigious of all is that of Prince Albert Victor, the Duke of Clarence.

At the time of the Ripper murders, Queen Victoria had been on the throne for over fifty years. Her immediate heir was her eldest son, who went on to succeed her as Edward VII when she died in 1901. The second in line to the throne was Edward's son – Prince Albert Victor. As it turned out, Albert Victor never lived to be King – he died of pneumonia in 1892 a few days after his 28th birthday. But in 1888, when five women were brutally murdered in Whitechapel, that still lay in the future.

Evidence connecting the Ripper murders with Albert Victor was uncovered in the 1960s by an elderly English doctor named Thomas Stowell – but Stowell died before he could disclose everything he knew. A few days after his death, all Stowell's documents and notes on the subject were destroyed by his son. So we are left with speculation – what was the connection between Prince Albert Victor and Jack the Ripper?

The commonest supposition is that the Ripper was a deranged madman with a deep hatred of women. Could this be the case with Albert Victor? Some authors have suggested the young Prince was driven mad by syphilis caught from a prostitute, and that this was the real cause of his premature death a few years later. If the authorities had known that Jack the Ripper was the second in line to the throne, they certainly would have done their best to cover it up. But the theory doesn't really hold water – there is no evidence that Albert Victor was mad, or that he had syphilis, or that he was even in London at the time of the murders.

There is another, more compelling, theory linking Queen Victoria's grandson to the Ripper murders. They may not have been the work of a madman at all, but of someone who knew exactly what he was doing. In this theory the victims were not chosen at random, but with calculated precision. They were women who knew too much – specifically, they knew that Prince Albert Victor had fathered an illegitimate child in the slums of the East End. For the British establishment, this was dangerous knowledge. It's possible the conspiracy went all the way to the top – to Queen Victoria and the Prime Minister of the time, Lord Salisbury.

In this case, there is no suggestion that the Prince himself committed the murders – he may have been blissfully unaware of them. So who was the perpetrator? Whoever it was, it's clear that he wanted to make the killings look like the work of a random madman – but he gave himself away in one key detail. The way the victims were mutilated shows a high degree of anatomical knowledge, indicating that the killer was a medical professional. One name that is often put forward is that of Sir William Gull, Queen Victoria's personal physician. Gull may indeed have been the mastermind behind the murders, but he was an old man at the time – so it's possible he left the dirty work to a more junior colleague.

God's second son (1851)

The bloodiest conflict in human history was the Taiping Rebellion, which took place in China in the 19th century. It resulted in the deaths of something like a hundred million people – close to a tenth of the world population at that time. Like Chairman Mao's revolution a hundred years later, the Taiping Rebellion sought to sweep aside China's established religions and replace them with something new. But in the case of the Taiping Rebellion, the new idea wasn't Communism – it was a strange, apocalyptic form of Christianity. Its leader, according to his own testimony, was none other than the younger brother of Jesus Christ.

Hong Xiuquan was born into a poor family in 1814. At the age of 23 he experienced a series of mystical visions, in which an old man gave him earnest instructions. Hong didn't understand the visions at the time, but on discovering some Christian writings a few years later he realized that the old man was God, and that he himself was God's second begotten son. It was his destiny to bring Christianity to China, and to rid the country of its "devils" – the traditional Chinese

Hong Xiuquan

gods and goddesses.

Hong started to preach his own peculiar version of Christianity, and gradually built up a following that became known as the God Worshippers. Initially the authorities put up with Hong and his followers, viewing them as harmless eccentrics. But by 1850 the movement had accumulated tens of thousands of members, and the government belatedly recognized the threat it posed to the country's stability. At the start of 1851, a detachment of Imperial troops was sent to deal with the God Worshippers, but it was too late – Hong's followers had become too powerful. The attacking troops were routed and their leader was beheaded.

Hong Xiuquan, the second son of God, promptly declared the inauguration of the Taiping Heavenly Kingdom. Taiping is a Chinese word meaning "great peace", although Hong's methods weren't entirely peaceful in the usual sense of the word. The civil war that followed, as already mentioned, was the bloodiest the world has ever seen. Hong established his Heavenly capital at Nanjing, while his reactionary enemies held on to the Imperial capital at Beijing. The deadly struggle between the Taiping Christians and the Chinese traditionalists tore the country apart for more than a dozen years.

Ironically, Hong's ultimate downfall came at the hands of Christians – albeit rather more orthodox ones than he himself was. An American soldier of fortune named Frederick Townsend Ward, seeing that the Chinese forces lacked organization and discipline, urged them to draft in officers from Europe to help pull them into shape. Under the leadership of Ward – and later of the

British General Charles Gordon – the Imperial forces managed to turn the tide. By August 1864 it was all over – the rebellion was crushed. Two months earlier, as he was facing certain defeat, Hong Xiuquan killed himself at his Heavenly Palace in Nanjing. General Gordon's troops were dubbed the Ever Victorious Army, and he became one of the few Englishmen to be hailed a hero of China.

Kaspar Hauser (1828)

In May 1828, a boy of about 17 appeared out of nowhere in the town of Nuremberg in Germany. He said his name was Kaspar Hauser, but that was virtually the only useful information he could provide. An anonymous letter he was carrying stated that Kaspar had been put in the writer's care as a baby on 7 October 1812, and that since that time he had been brought up in virtual isolation from the outside world.

The story of Kaspar Hauser caused a sensation at the time. Some people accused him of being an attention-seeking fraud, while others took his story at face value. He stuck to it doggedly for five years, until he was stabbed to death by person or persons unknown. His mysterious murder, and his strangely secretive upbringing, led many people to speculate that he was the child of a noble family that someone wanted out of the way.

One possibility is that Kaspar was the Grand Duke of Baden's son, who had been born on 29 September 1812 and supposedly died a few weeks later. The theory is that, rather than dying, the boy was abducted and imprisoned. If this was true, then Kaspar should have inherited the dukedom when his father died in 1818. As it was, though, the title passed sideways to another branch of the family. One of the chief beneficiaries was the Countess of Hochberg, who many people consider the most likely suspect in the case. Recent DNA tests have given tantalizing hints of a link between Kaspar Hauser and the Baden family.

The Count of Saint Germain (1745)

The Count of Saint Germain is one of the most enigmatic figures in history. The oldest surviving reference to him occurs in a letter written in 1745 by the English novelist Horace Walpole, who describes Saint Germain as an "odd man" who was arrested in London as a spy but later released when nothing was found to incriminate him. According to Walpole, the Count "will not tell who he is or whence" and "does not go by his right name". Even in those early days, speculation was rife: "He is called an Italian, a Spaniard, a Pole, a somebody that married a great fortune in Mexico, and ran away with her jewels to Constantinople, a priest, a fiddler, a vast nobleman. The Prince of Wales has had unsatiated curiosity about him, but in vain."

When he appeared in London, Saint Germain was working as a musician – he gave concerts and composed at least 50 pieces of music. Twelve years later, however, his career changed track and he became an inventor. He visited the French King Louis XV in Paris, trying to interest him in a new dye-making process. Louis was less interested in the invention than in the man himself, though, and the Count soon became a member of the King's inner circle. He amazed everyone with his mastery of languages – there were at least ten he could speak fluently – and his vast knowledge of history. He claimed to be hundreds of years old – possibly only as a joke, although the claim was taken seriously by some people at the time.... as it still is today.

From France the Count travelled to Russia, where his interests apparently shifted once again – this time from chemistry to politics. It's alleged that he helped Catherine the Great in her overthrow of Peter III, which was described in the previous chapter. On his return to western Europe a few years later, however, he was back to his chemical processes... with one important difference. He'd moved on from dyeing fabrics – now he said he could transmute base metals into gold. The

Count of Saint Germain had become an alchemist.

According to the official view, the Count finally died in Germany in 1784. Many people, however, claimed to meet him after that – never looking much older than 45. Sightings continued well into the 20th century, when Saint Germain became something of a cult figure among New Agers and occultists.

Legends aside, there are some real mysteries surrounding the Count of Saint Germain. It's obvious he was a very talented individual, but where did he come from? He admitted he wasn't using his real name, and he was notoriously secretive about his early life and upbringing. So why were people like Louis XV of France and Catherine the Great of Russia – two of the most powerful people in the world – happy to treat the man as a near-equal? The obvious answer is that they knew his real identity, and he was someone important. One possibility came from the mouth of the Count himself. Towards the end of his life he claimed to be the eldest son of a former ruler of Transylvania named Francis II Rákóczi. That may have been true – or then again, given the many conflicting statements he uttered over the years, it may not.

The Shakespeare mystery (1604)

William Shakespeare is probably the best known writer in the English language. He was one of the leading poets and playwrights of the late Elizabethan and early Jacobean period, and his name would have been familiar to everyone in London society at the time – including Queen Elizabeth I and her successor King James I. Yet there is an enduring mystery about Shakespeare. Documentary evidence about the man – as opposed to his works – is hard to come by. Records from Shakespeare's lifetime are consistent with his being a middle-class businessman – not a towering literary figure.

There's no doubt Shakespeare was a middle-class businessman, of course. He was a partner in one of London's leading theatrical companies as well as an actor in it. Many of the plays performed by the company bore Shakespeare's name as author. But did he really write them, or was his name just a convenient cover for someone else? Over the years, many people have suggested the latter was the case – including prominent figures such as Sigmund Freud, who wrote in his autobiography "I no longer believe that the actor from Stratford was the author of the works that have been ascribed to him."

If Shakespeare didn't write his plays, then who did? Several possible contenders have been put forward. One of them was mentioned in the previous chapter – Christopher Marlowe. If Marlowe faked his own death in 1593, in order to avoid being executed for treason, then what did he do for the rest of his life? It's reasonable to suppose he continued to do what he did best – write plays. Shakespeare was the same age as Marlowe, but up to the time of Marlowe's supposed death his plays were distinctly inferior. It was only after 1593 that he became a big-name author.

The name that is most often put forward as the true author of Shakespeare's plays is Edward de Vere, the 17th Earl of Oxford. An Earl is a senior member of the nobility – the British equivalent of a Count in other countries. An Earl should have been above the writing of mere entertainments – so the theory goes – and hence he was forced to use a pseudonym. The supporting evidence is essentially biographical – there are many characters, settings and incidents in Shakespeare's plays that seem to match up with the Earl's own experience. The problem, however, lies in the chronology. The Earl was already in his forties when the first Shakespeare plays were written, and at least ten of them appear to have been produced after he died in 1604 – they even contain topical references to events after that date.

Another suggestion is that the plays were the work of the philosopher Sir Francis Bacon, who was born just three years before Shakespeare. Unlike the Earl of Oxford, Bacon is one of the great figures of history. He was a pioneer of the scientific method – which prior to the 20th century was referred to as the Baconian method. Bacon was an advocate of practical experimentation – he was the first person to demonstrate that meat could be preserved by freezing, for example... although he died from pneumonia in the process. But that was more than ten years after the last of Shakespeare's plays had appeared, so the Baconian theory doesn't have the chronological problem that the Oxfordian theory does.

Another passion of Bacon's was cryptography – he invented a number of secret coding methods. Intriguingly, some of the strongest evidence for his authorship of Shakespeare's plays comes from supposed cryptograms they contain.

The Man in the Iron Mask (1669)

King Louis XIV ruled over France for 72 years, from 1643 – when he was just four years old – until his death in 1715. For almost half that time, Louis kept a mysterious prisoner locked up. The man was arrested in 1669, and initially incarcerated in the fortress of Pignerol which was reserved for dangerous political prisoners. He died in another notorious French prison, the Bastille, 34 years later. No-one knows who the man was, because no-one ever saw his face. He may not actually have worn an iron mask – some accounts say it was a mask of black velvet – but he did go through his entire captivity with his face covered.

The fact that he was held in high security jails suggests the prisoner posed a serious risk to the state. The fact that he was imprisoned, rather than being executed, suggests that he was more valuable alive than dead. Finally, the fact that he was forced to wear a mask suggests that his face was instantly recognizable, or that he closely resembled someone else.

Making sense of these apparently conflicting facts isn't easy. The most likely explanation is that the prisoner was a close relative of Louis XIV – possibly one with a stronger claim to the throne... or who knew that the King's own claim to it was illegitimate.

Richard the Fourth (1497)

After Richard III was killed at the Battle of Bosworth Field in 1485, the leader of the opposing forces – a Welsh nobleman named Henry Tudor – was crowned King Henry VII. His hereditary claim to the throne was indirect to say the least, but it was less indirect than anyone else's. Richard III died without any legitimate heirs, and his predecessor – his older brother Edward IV – also left no surviving male heirs. His two sons, Edward and Richard, disappeared in mysterious circumstances soon after his death in 1483.

Richard III was supposed to look after the boys, who were only 12 and 9 years old at the time of their father's death. Instead, he locked them in the Tower of London, and after a few months they were never seen again. No-one knows what happened to the Princes in the Tower – the usual assumption is that Richard either murdered them or allowed them to die from neglect. If so, then his aim was to secure the throne for himself – with the two boys out of the way, he was next in line. As it turned out, though, the real winner was not Richard – who only reigned for two years – but Henry Tudor, who reigned for 24.

Henry's reign was not without incident, however. He was deeply unpopular in parts of the country, particularly Cornwall, where there were mutterings of rebellion. In 1497, a young man arrived on the Cornish coast with a small force of armed men. He claimed to be Richard, Duke of York – the younger of the two Princes in the Tower. The people of Cornwall, fed up with the King they had, agreed to help him regain the throne.

His army augmented by thousands of Tudor-hating Cornishmen, the claimant to the throne marched eastwards. On Bodmin Moor, he was crowned King Richard IV. The first city he came to was Exeter, and that's where his plan started to go awry. He was forced to back off by troops loyal to the King, so he headed for Taunton in Somerset instead. When he got there, he found that more of the King's troops were approaching from the other direction. He was rapidly becoming hemmed in. Deciding that discretion was the better part of valour, King Richard IV promptly deserted his own army. He fled to Hampshire and took refuge in Beaulieu Abbey.

Eventually the fugitive was discovered and persuaded to surrender. Under torture, he confessed to being an impostor – a commoner named Perkin Warbeck who had no valid claim to the throne. He was taken to London, where he was locked up in the Tower for two years before finally being executed.

There's no doubt that Perkin Warbeck's rebellion was a badly organized shambles, but was he really an impostor? Or was he the rightful heir to the throne, just as he originally claimed to be? It was only under torture that he went back on this story, and torture is a notoriously unreliable way of extracting the truth. If the torturer wants you to say you're an impostor, then sooner or later you will say you're an impostor. It was in Henry VII's interest, after all, to get rid of any remaining sons of Edward IV... just as it had been in Richard III's interest 14 years earlier.

The Green Children (1173)

Woolpit is a small village in Suffolk, which gets its name from the wolf-pits that used to be dug in the area to trap wolves. Around the year 1173, something was found in one of the pits that was not a wolf. It was a pair of young children – a boy and a girl – and they were both green. The locals were baffled – the children spoke a strange language, and there was no clue as to how they got there.

Soon after they were found the boy became ill and died, but the girl survived. She lost her green colour, learned to speak English, and was adopted by a well-to-do local family. But she was never able to explain where she came from.

Nowadays, if green people suddenly appeared out of nowhere, sooner or later someone would suggest they came from another planet. But in the 12th century, that wasn't an option. No-one had seen a planet through a telescope, so no-one had any idea those little lights in the sky might be other worlds like the Earth. It was only in the time of Galileo that this began to dawn on people. As soon as it did, someone made the connection. The *Anatomy of Melancholy* was written by an Englishman named Robert Burton in 1621, soon after Galileo's discoveries were made public. In a chapter dealing with astronomy, after Burton points out that the other planets might be inhabited, he adds "it may be those two green children that fell from heaven, came from thence."

Other more mundane suggestions have been put forward. At the time of the children's appearance, England was in the throes of rebellion. The reign of King Henry II was challenged, not by outsiders, but by his own wife and children. In October 1173 a battle took place at Fornham less than ten miles from Woolpit, between Royalist forces and rebels supported by a large number of Flemish mercenaries. The Battle of Fornham was a rout – the rebels were defeated and thousands of Flemish soldiers were killed. Given the proximity in time and space, it's possible there's a connection between the battle and the green children. They may have belonged to Flemish mercenaries who lost their lives in the fighting. That would explain why they spoke a foreign language – but it wouldn't explain why they were green... unless, of course, "green" was simply a description of the clothes they were wearing.

Although convenient, the explanation doesn't ring true – foreign mercenaries don't usually take their children into battle with them. Also, it doesn't explain the reverence with which the surviving child – the girl – was treated. It's said the King himself took an interest in her well-being, and she was placed in the care of one of his most trusted aides – a man who happened to be a member of the secretive Knights Templar. Later, the girl appears to have married one of the King's senior ambassadors. That seems an unlikely outcome if she was nothing more than the orphan of an enemy soldier – but just who she really was, no-one knows to this day.

A young pretender (1487)

Ten years before Perkin Warbeck's rebellion, Henry VII had to deal with another pretender to the throne. This was a rather different situation, though. Warbeck, whether he was an impostor or the real thing, was the instigator of his own rebellion. In the earlier case, however, the claimant to the throne was a ten year old boy named Lambert Simnel. He was just a puppet in the affair, selected because his facial features resembled those of the royal family. The brains behind the plot was Simnel's tutor – a man named Richard Symonds. He tried to pass the young boy off as a nephew of Richard III, who had a stronger claim to the throne that Henry VII himself.

Symonds managed to pull together a sizeable army to support his claim, but they were defeated at the Battle of Stoke Field in June 1487. Henry VII doesn't seem to have taken this attempt on his throne very seriously, though – Richard Symonds was merely imprisoned, not executed, while the young Lambert Simnel was given a job in the King's service.

Chapter 7: The Illuminati and others

The Priory of Sion (1967)

A common thread running through modern conspiracy theories is the idea of a powerful elite that has existed in the shadows for centuries. One of the best known, thanks to Dan Brown's 2003 novel *The Da Vinci Code*, is the Priory of Sion. In the novel, the Priory exists to preserve a dangerous secret – that Jesus Christ survived the crucifixion, married Mary Magdalene, and spawned a bloodline than exists to the present day. Parts of this story, at least, can trace their origins to an apparent hoax.

Two critical events occurred in 1967. A right-wing French activist named Pierre Plantard deposited a document known as the *Dossiers Secrets* in the national library in Paris. The same year, a friend of Plantard's named Gérard de Sède wrote a book whose title translates as "The Accursed Treasure of Rennes-le-Château". Together, the document and the book contain many of the incidental details associated with the Priory of Sion – that it stretches back to the time of the Crusades, that it was charged with guarding an important secret, that one of its grand masters was Leonardo Da Vinci, and that the secret was unearthed by a priest in the small village of Rennes-le-Chateau in the 19th century.

There is strong evidence, however, that the *Dossiers Secrets* was a fake concocted by Plantard himself, and that he provided de Sède with the salient facts for his book – which are equally fake. There is nothing in Plantard's version about Jesus or Mary Magdalene – the focus is on the bloodline of the French royal family, and Plantard's aim appears to have been to establish himself as the rightful heir to the throne.

The Priory of Sion's controversial Biblical connections were unleashed in a later book, *The Holy Blood and the Holy Grail*, published in 1982. The authors were an Englishman, a New Zealander and an American, who had no great interest in the French royal family or the particular brand of right-wing politics espoused by Plantard. Instead, their target was the Roman Catholic Church, which becomes the villain in their version of events – which is ironic, because Plantard himself was a Roman Catholic.

When Prophecy Fails (1954)

The 1950s saw the rise of a number of "flying saucer cults" that combined a belief in extraterrestrials with apocalyptic religious ideas. One such cult in America was led by a female psychic, who received a message telling her that God was going to destroy the world on 21 December 1954. Fortunately, a flying saucer from the planet Clarion would come to rescue the cult members at midnight on the previous day.

The cultists gave away all their worldly possessions and waited for their deliverance. But the aliens didn't come to rescue them... and the world didn't end the following day. The leader received another message saying that God had decided to give the world a second chance. The end result was that, following the failed prophecy, most of the cult members became more fervent believers – not less.

The case was written up by a psychologist named Leon Festinger in a book entitled *When Prophecy Fails*. Festinger coined the term "cognitive dissonance" to describe the inner conflict that causes devout believers to interpret any new evidence – positive or negative – as reinforcing their beliefs.

Despite its murky history, many people today continue to take the Priory of Sion at face value – the version as presented in *The Da Vinci Code* and *The Holy Blood and the Holy Grail*, that is. Plantard's work wasn't the only source for this, and there may be some underlying truth to it. But the fact remains that at least some of the currently accepted details have been exposed as originating in a hoax.

The official emblem used by the Priory of Sion.

This is the point at which the idea of a shadowy, all-powerful elite really comes into its own. If such an elite exists, as many people believe, then it will have the power and influence to alter the historical audit trail to suit its own ends. If a document appears to be forged, it's because they wanted it to appear to be forged. If historical records contradict the theory, that's because the records have been tampered with. A conspiracy involving a secret elite is virtually impossible to disprove – and that's one of the reasons they feature so prominently in most modern conspiracy theories.

The Bible and the British monarchy (1885)

Books like The Da Vinci Code and The Holy Blood and the Holy Grail have popularized the idea that French royalty can trace its roots to Biblical times. But similar claims have been made for the British royal family. In 1885, the Reverend A. B. Grimaldi produced a genealogical table showing how Queen Victoria, who was reigning at the time, was descended from the Biblical kings of Judah.

According to the Old Testament the last king of Judah was Zedekiah, whose reign ended in 587 BC following the fall of Jerusalem to the Babylonians. Zedekiah left no male heirs, but legend says he had one surviving daughter named Tea Tephi. She fled by sea to Ireland, where she married King Heremon. The descendants of Heremon and Tea Tephi held onto the Irish throne through the generations, and in 487 King Fergus the Great became King of Scotland as well. All the subsequent Scottish monarchs were descended from him, until in 1603 King James VI of Scotland became King James I of England. The continuation of the bloodline all the way to the Royal Family of today is known to every school child.

The Reverend Grimaldi was consolidating a view that had emerged earlier in the 19th century – that Britain's monarchs could trace their ancestry to the Kings of Judah. But the broad idea that the British are connected in some way to people mentioned in the Bible goes back further than that. In the early 16th century, a man named William Tyndale translated the Bible into English. He wasn't the first person to do this, but he was the first to translate it from the original texts – not indirectly from a Latin translation. In the case of the Old Testament, this meant translating from Hebrew – the scriptural language of the ancient Israelites. Tyndale was astonished to find that for every word in the English language that was derived from Latin, there were a thousand words derived from Hebrew. Modern readers may consider this an exaggeration, but to Tyndale it was clear evidence that the British were descended, not from continental Europeans, but from the Biblical Israelites.

For much of the period covered by the Old Testament, there were two Hebrew-speaking kingdoms – Judah in the south and Israel in the north. The descendants of Judah survive to this day in the form of the Jewish people. But what of ancient Israel? According to the Biblical account, the kingdom was conquered by the Assyrians in 722 BC and its inhabitants became dispersed. As to what happened to them subsequently, the Bible is silent – they are commonly referred to as the "Lost Tribes of Israel".

With the rise of Protestantism in the English-speaking world, an increasing emphasis was put on the Old Testament. But what was its special relevance to English-speaking people? Maybe they were the Lost Tribes! A belief grew up that some of the exiled Israelites found their way to the British Isles and to North America. The movement became known as "British Israelism", although it was at least as prevalent in the United States as in Britain.

Mozart and the Freemasons (1791)

The composer Wolfgang Amadeus Mozart became a Freemason at the age of 28 in 1784. Then as now, Freemasonry was treated with suspicion by many people. After all, it was a secret society that was selective in who it admitted, and people on the outside were denied any knowledge of what went on inside. Today's suspicions revolve around the supposed political aspirations of the Masons – in the 18th century the focus was on their religious views. Freemasons believe in God... but not necessarily the God of Christianity.

The religious aspects of Freemasonry particularly appealed to Mozart. He wrote musical pieces for Masonic gatherings, which contained references to Hindu and Chinese deities as well as the Judaeo-Christian one. September 1791 saw the first performance of *The Magic Flute* – the opera many people consider to be his masterpiece – which is filled with Masonic symbolism, from secret rituals to hymns extolling the gods and goddesses of ancient Egypt.

Two months later, Mozart was dead. The fact that he was only 35 years old, and that his death has never been adequately explained, has led many people to speculate that he was murdered. If so, did this have any connection with *The Magic Flute*? The opera may have antagonized the Masonic community – for revealing their rituals and incantations – or fanatical Christians who were offended by its heretical nature.

The real Illuminati (1776)

Modern conspiracy theorists refer to the secret group that supposedly controls world affairs by various names, one of the best known being the Illuminati. This name comes from a Latin word meaning "the enlightened ones", and the original Illuminati emerged during the 18th century out of an intellectual movement of the period known as the Enlightenment.

The basic principles of the Enlightenment were ones that few people today would disagree with – that rationality is superior to superstition, that science is a higher authority than religion, and that power should reside with individual citizens rather than a powerful church or state. These were the values espoused by the original Illuminati, formed as a secret society by Adam Weishaupt in 1776. The society originated in Bavaria, so it is often referred to as the Bavarian Illuminati to distinguish it from later organizations that have adopted the same name.

From the start, there was a contradiction at the heart of the Bavarian Illuminati. On the one hand they espoused values such as freedom, openness and democracy. On the other, they were a secret society that was only accessible to the chosen few. As a general rule, people don't like secret societies. If they're secret, they must be doing something sinister. This argument applied to the Bavarian Illuminati as much as any other secret society, and they were outlawed by the Duke of Bavaria just eight years after their formation.

That was in 1785. Four years later, and 800 kilometres to the west, the French Revolution erupted in Paris. The beliefs of the revolutionaries were identical to those of the Illuminati – but their methods were brutal in the extreme. Tens of thousands of aristocrats were slaughtered in the name of freedom and equality. Outside France, the Revolution was viewed with horror – not least because its perpetrators openly espoused atheism.

Arguably the first modern-style conspiracy theory emerged soon afterwards – that the Bavarian Illuminati had secretly engineered the French Revolution to further their own agenda. This view was first articulated by a Scotsman named John Robison. He wasn't a crank or a social misfit – he was a professor of philosophy at Edinburgh University. He started out as an advocate of the Enlightenment, but after the excesses of the French Revolution he began to have second thoughts.

In 1797 Robison published a book with the rather wordy title "Proofs of a Conspiracy against all the Religions and Governments of Europe, carried on in the secret meetings of Freemasons,

Illuminati and Reading Societies". Significantly the title includes the word "conspiracy" and pins the blame on secret societies – the Illuminati among them. It was Robison's contention that, far from being disbanded, the Bavarian Illuminati teamed up with the Freemasons and other secret societies to reshape Europe into the form they wanted. The French Revolution was just the first step in the process.

Robison may have been right – or he may have been wrong. There's little doubt that the French Revolution, while presented as a populist uprising, was actually the brainchild of a small number of intellectuals. Whether this was the Illuminati – or any other clandestine elite with an ulterior agenda – is another matter, however.

The Fifth Monarchists (1653)

Religious cults whose members believe in the imminent end of the world have always existed. Usually they inhabit the fringes of society, and their beliefs are ridiculed by the mainstream establishment. But in 1653, one such cult managed to take control of a whole country for a period of six months. The country in question was England.

After the execution of King Charles I in 1649, both the monarchy and the House of Lords were abolished. England was ruled by the House of Commons. In the wake of Pride's Purge, which was covered in Chapter 4, only about 70 members of Parliament remained active. While they all agreed that getting rid of the King was a good idea, they didn't necessarily agree about anything else. By 1653 the situation was starting to annoy Oliver Cromwell, who had risen to be the most powerful voice in Parliament by that time. How was he expected to get anything done if people insisted on arguing all the time?

Cromwell's patience finally ran out on 20 April. Addressing the House of Commons, he made what may be the least weasel-worded speech that chamber has ever witnessed: "Ye sordid prostitutes, have you not defiled this sacred place and turned the

Lord's temple into a den of thieves? Ye are grown intolerably odious to the whole nation. You were deputed here by the people to get grievances redressed, and yourselves become the greatest grievance. I command ye therefore, upon the peril of your lives, to depart immediately out of this place. Go, get you out! In the name of God, go!"

They went. Cromwell now had an empty chamber, which he was going to fill with people who would do things the way he wanted. This was the point at which the religious cult entered the picture. They called themselves the Fifth Monarchists, because they believed themselves to be heralds of the fifth world-spanning monarchy – nothing short of the Kingdom of Christ on Earth. The first four monarchies, which had been prophesied in the Biblical Book of Daniel, had already come and gone.

The leader of the cult was a man with the unlikely-sounding name of Praise-God Barebone. His parents had been Puritans – hence the name – but he went a step further. He believed he was the first saint of the Kingdom of Heaven. Barebone's Parliament was installed on 4 July 1653 and promptly took over the running, if not of the Kingdom of Heaven, then at least of the Commonwealth of England.

Several problems became apparent fairly quickly. To start with, the Fifth Monarchists had no idea how to run a country. Secondly, the population of England – for some unaccountable reason – found it impossible to take their new Parliament seriously. Finally, the cultists spent just as much time sitting around arguing as their predecessors had. As far as Cromwell was concerned, this last point was the worst of all. It was a case of déjà vu – and his solution this time was the same as it had been on the previous occasion. On 12 December 1653, after just six months, the Barebone's Parliament was dissolved.

Four days later Oliver Cromwell became Lord Protector of England. If no-one else could do the job properly, he was going to do it himself.

The School of Night (1592)

The mysterious death of the playwright Christopher Marlowe was described in Chapter 5. One of the charges against him was that he was an atheist – which was a serious crime in Elizabethan England. Some people believe he was a member of a shadowy organization called the School of Night, which existed to undermine church and state. This may or may not be true – unambiguous evidence is hard to come by, as might be expected in the case of a secret society. Being accused of atheism in 1590s England was like being accused of Communism in 1950s America. On the one hand, the movement was espoused by many intellectuals of the time – but on the other, it was a useful pejorative to deploy against an enemy even if they were completely innocent of the charge.

The alleged ringleader of the School of Night was Sir Walter Raleigh, the famous explorer who helped to establish the colony of Virginia, and introduced tobacco-smoking to Europe. Another prominent member was an astronomer named Thomas Heriot. Although few people today have heard of him, he was an English contemporary of Galileo who was equally revolutionary in his views.

Treasonable necromancy (1441)

In the popular imagination, the Middle Ages were filled with witches and sorcerers. While such people did exist, they usually worked in the shadows and had little impact on the unfolding of history. There was one notable exception in 15th century England, however, when the arcane world of sorcery and witchcraft clashed with the practical world of politics.

The instigator of the event was a prominent noblewoman – Eleanor, Duchess of Gloucester. She probably wasn't a witch or sorceress herself, although she is sometimes described as such. It's more likely that she was simply a highly ambitious individual who was prepared to use any methods at her disposal. As a young woman in the 1420s, she secured a position as an aide to the Duke of Gloucester's wife. The Duke of Gloucester effectively ruled the country, as guardian to his nephew Henry VI – who, although he was nominally King of England, was only a child at the time.

Being an aide to the wife of the most powerful man in the country wasn't good enough for Eleanor. In 1428 the Duke of Gloucester's marriage was annulled, and Eleanor became his new wife. She was Duchess of Gloucester – consort of England's *de facto* ruler – and that suited her ambitions perfectly. But it wasn't going to last forever. Eventually Henry VI would reach maturity and take over the running of the country.

It's at this point that witchcraft and sorcery enter the picture. In 1441, when the King was 19 years old, Eleanor decided she needed a clearer view of the future. She consulted with three members of her staff, all of whom had a more than passing familiarity with the occult arts – her clerk Roger Bolingbroke, her personal physician Thomas Southwell and her priest John Hume. Also on hand was an out-and-out witch – a woman named Margery Jourdain, who was well known at the time as the "Witch of Eye".

The four of them – Bolingbroke, Southwell, Hume and Jourdain – produced a horoscope which appeared to foretell the death of the King within a matter of months. This was great news for Eleanor, because her husband was next in line to the throne. With Henry's death, the Duke of Gloucester would become King... and Eleanor would be Queen. But things didn't go the way she would have liked. When the King's spies heard about the prophecy, it was interpreted as an attempt to bring about his premature death by means of witchcraft.

The five conspirators were put on trial, and found guilty of treasonable necromancy. Margery Jourdain was burned at the stake on 27 October 1441, and three weeks later Roger Bolingbroke was hung, drawn and quartered. The other conspirators, including Eleanor, avoided the death sentence – although she spent the rest of her life in prison.

The Knights Templar (1307)

By the end of the 11th century, following the first Crusade, the city of Jerusalem and much of the surrounding "Holy Land" was in the hands of European Christendom. But it was under constant threat from Islamic forces in the surrounding areas. In order to protect Christian interests in and around Jerusalem, a number of resident military orders were established during the course of the 12th century. The best known of these was the Order of the Temple.

The stated mission of the Knights Templar – to protect Christians visiting the Holy Land – may seem straightforward enough, yet they went on to become one of the most mysterious and controversial organizations in history. From the start, the Templars were unusual in several ways. Their role was military, but their organization was monastic – the first "fighting monks" the world had ever seen. They were one of the first genuinely international organizations – their members were drawn from all the countries of Europe, they didn't have to pay local taxes or obey local laws, and they were answerable only to the Pope. Perhaps most significantly of all, the Templars were the first Europeans since the time of the Roman Empire to spend their entire lives steeped in a non-European culture.

The Templars may or may not have been swayed by Islamic beliefs, but there's no doubt they were influenced by Islamic culture. They gained knowledge in practical areas like science, architecture and engineering – and, according to some accounts, dangerously esoteric knowledge as well. There are endless speculations about what the Templars may or may not have discovered while they were based in Jerusalem. Did they unearth mystical artifacts like the Holy Grail or the Ark of the Covenant? One thing is certain, though – during the course of their existence, the Knights Templar amassed an enormous amount of wealth.

Wealth leads to power. By the 13th century the Templars had acquired vast tracts of land all across Europe, as well as controlling the continent's financial infrastructure. When they were finally forced out of the Holy Land and they returned to Europe, their power rivalled that of any kingdom.

The Templars' power came to an abrupt end in 1307, when Pope Clement V outlawed the order and had its members arrested on charges of heresy. Many of them were tortured – resulting in bizarre confessions of unholy acts – and burnt at the stake. The brutal suppression of the Knights Templar, instead of dispersing the myths surrounding them, only served to reinforce speculation. Although powerful, the Templars were answerable to the Pope. If he merely wanted to disband them because they were becoming so powerful, he had the perfect excuse for doing so. Their mission to the Holy Land had failed, so their services were no longer required. He could simply have given them their statutory month's notice and ordered them to return all their assets to the Church. But he didn't do that – he chose to persecute them, torture them and execute them.

If the Templars really were preaching heresy – by openly promoting a form of Islam, for example – then the Pope's actions might have been justified within the prevailing standards of the time. But there's no real evidence, apart from confessions extracted under torture, that the Templars were heretics. So the explanation for the Pope's actions has to be sought elsewhere... and there is no shortage of conspiracy theories on the subject. Some are relatively mundane, such as the suggestion that the Templars' persecution had nothing to do with religion and everything to do with politics – the Pope's hand may have been forced by the King of France, for example. At the other extreme, there are all the rumours about the Holy Grail, the Ark of the Covenant and other dark secrets. The truth, as with all good conspiracies, will probably never be known.

Mystery cult (186 BC)

Ancient Greece and Rome had their own secret societies in the form of so-called mystery religions. Unlike the conventional religions of the time, these were only open to people who had been specially selected and initiated into the "mystery" – usually people of high social rank. Their rituals were conducted in secret, and the details were passed on from one initiate to another rather than being written down. For this reason it's difficult to know exactly what went on, although the rituals may have had similarities to those of the Freemasons today. While the mystery religions nominally worshipped gods and goddesses, their adherents were intellectually sophisticated enough to view such deities as symbolic rather than real.

One of the most notorious mystery religions centred on the god Dionysus, also known as Bacchus in Roman times. Usually described as the "God of Wine", this may have been a euphemism for something a little stronger. Many of the mystery cults are believed to have used entheogenic drugs – psychoactive substances that are reputed to be capable of triggering mystical experiences in the user.

Whether the Dionysian rituals used wine or another drug, the group celebrations that followed became notorious for their unbridled nature. Called Bacchanalia, they were described by the Roman historian Livy as follows: "Men mingled with women with all the licence of nocturnal orgies; there was no crime, no deed of shame, wanting. More uncleanness was wrought by men with men than with women. Whoever would not submit to defilement, or shrank from violating others, was sacrificed as a victim. To regard nothing as impious or criminal was the very sum of their religion."

Not surprisingly, the Bacchanalia were viewed with concern by the authorities. The followers of Dionysus were increasingly seen as a threat to state security, and in 186 BC the Roman senate issued a decree making the cult illegal. Thousands of its members were executed and all its shrines were destroyed. This wasn't the end of the Dionysian religion, however. The movement was forced underground, and Dionysus became a symbol of rebellion against Roman rule. Mithridates, King of Pontus, who fought against the Romans a hundred years later, considered himself to be the living incarnation of Dionysus... as did the gladiator Spartacus who led the slave revolt of 73 BC.

Chapter 8: Rewriting history

Soviet censorship (1940)

To most people, history is a succession of events that are caused either by random chance or by the actions and/or errors of individual human beings. But to Karl Marx, the 19th century pioneer of Communism, history was something else entirely. It was an ordered, logical progression from a world of oppressive capitalism to one of peace-loving, tree-hugging Communism. Marx referred to this process as Dialectical Materialism.

There's just one small problem with Dialectical Materialism – no-one bothered to tell history that's what it was supposed to be doing. For this reason, Communist states have often found it necessary to alter the historic record in order to make it fit the theory. This was particularly true in the Soviet Union during the period that Joseph Stalin was its leader, between 1922 and 1952. The Communists came to power in Russia following the October Revolution of 1917. This was led by Vladimir Lenin, supported by other senior Communists including Stalin. By the time of Lenin's death early in 1924, Stalin was already installed as head of the Soviet Union. But a document came to light called "Lenin's Testament", which the revolutionary leader had written when he knew he was going to die. Amongst other things, the document ordered that Stalin should be removed from power.

This was obviously a mistake. Stalin tried to suppress the document, but news of its existence leaked out and it was published in the *New York Times* in 1926. Within the Soviet Union, however, the document's existence continued to be denied, and any reference to it was considered "anti-Soviet agitation" and a criminal offence.

Leon Trotsky was another person who had been involved in the October Revolution. He was a Communist, like Lenin and Stalin, but he was a reactionary one. In terms of Dialectical Materialism, this meant he wanted history to go backwards instead of forwards. In simpler terms, it meant he disagreed with Stalin. Whichever way you look at it, Leon Trotsky was another of history's mistakes.

Trotsky was declared an enemy of the Soviet Union and expelled from the country. Stalin's historians then set about erasing all records of Trotsky's life and work – they were going to make it look like he had never existed. His role in the Revolution was edited out of the history books, and his image was airbrushed out of official photographs.

The original version of this photo taken in 1939 shows Stalin with Yezhov, but the version releasted in 1941 has Yezhov painted out.

This was just the start of it. Airbrushing people out of history was too good an idea to use it just once. During the 1930s, Stalin ordered a Great Purge of all the reactionaries who were holding back the tide of progress. Something like half the entire Soviet political and military establishment was imprisoned or shot, and their existence wiped from the history books.

The official in charge of the purges was a man named Nikolai Yezhov, who was the People's Commissar for State Security. This was a powerful position – too powerful for his own good, in fact. On 2 February 1940 Yezhov was put on trial as an enemy of the people, and two days later he was executed. Ironically, Yezhov's ultimate fate was the same as that of his victims – he was airbrushed out of history. His disappearance from official photographs has led to the nickname "the Vanishing Commissar" among historians.

The past according to the Nazis (1935)

The Nazi party swept to power in 1933 on a wave of German nationalism. This was a matter of historical pride – the Germans knew they'd always been the greatest nation on Earth. Unfortunately, the historic record – as it stood at the time – was noticeably incomplete. The Germans didn't feature very prominently at all. The British did, and the French, and the Spanish, and the Italians, and the Greeks, and the Persians, and the Egyptians... and even the Jews. But not the Germans. Obviously something needed to be done about the situation.

In 1935 a special organization was set up called *Deutsches Ahnenerbe*, meaning "German Heritage". Like all the crankiest ideas of the Third Reich, this fell under the auspices of Reichsführer-SS Heinrich Himmler. The aims of the *Ahnenerbe* were essentially twofold: first, to prove that world civilization originated in the part of Europe that is now Germany, and secondly, to prove that if it didn't start there but somewhere else, then the people who started it were Germans anyhow.

During the 19th century linguists noticed that German has more in common with Sanskrit, the scriptural language of ancient India, than it does with Hebrew, the scriptural language of Judaism. Languages derived from Sanskrit were dubbed Aryan, from a Sanskrit word meaning "noble", while those related to Hebrew were called Semitic, after the Biblical figure of Shem from whom all Hebrew-speaking people are supposed to be descended.

To the Nazis, this was too good an idea to pass up – after all, militant anti-Semitism lay at the very heart of their policies. They saw the whole of history as a struggle between the Aryan-speaking peoples of the world – who they believed came from the lost continent of Atlantis – and the supposedly inferior Semitic-speaking peoples.

The fact that Aryan was an Indian word suggested, to the Nazi way of thinking, that the ancient Indians must really have been Germans. For example, the Buddha – in the 6th century BC – had referred to himself as an Aryan, which meant he must have been a direct ancestor of modern Germans. This was good news – it pushed German history back to the very origins of civilization, which had been the objective all along. Adding an Indian dimension would have a practical benefit, too – the Nazis and the Indian nationalists shared a common enemy in the form of the British Empire. The Indians, however, were not as impressed by the German theories as the Germans themselves were.

One of the most bizarre undertakings of the Nazi era was the SS-sponsored expedition to Tibet in 1939 – the year the Second World War broke out. Organized by the Ahnenerbe, the expedition's main aim was to prove that the distant Himalayan country had, thousands of years earlier, been occupied by pure-bred Aryans indistinguishable from modern-day Germans. After extensive data collection, the members of the expedition succeeded in validating the theory to their own satisfaction... but not anyone else's.

The Indemnity and Oblivion Act (1660)

Between the execution of Charles I in 1649 and the restoration of Charles II in 1660, England didn't have a King. In retrospect, this period is referred to as the Interregnum – a Latin word meaning "between the reigns". After Parliament restored Charles II to the throne, one of the first laws he was asked to pass was the Indemnity and Oblivion Act of 1660. The main purpose of the Act was to grant immunity from prosecution to anyone who had held office during the Interregnum, with the exception of those who had actively been involved in the execution of Charles I. That was the "indemnity" part.

The "oblivion" part of the Act was a rather more bizarre piece of legislature. It made it a criminal offence, for a period of three years from the date of the Act, for anyone to refer to the fact that the Interregnum had taken place. The penalty for violating this injunction was a fine of ten pounds for the gentry, or two pounds for the working classes. Although many politicians over the years have tried to suppress historical facts, the Indemnity and Oblivion Act may be the only time it was enshrined in law!

The Papal prophecies (1590)

An interesting variation on the theme of "rewriting history" occurred in 1590. The history that was being rewritten in this case wasn't in the past but the future. The focus of the exercise was a prophecy that had supposedly been written down by Saint Malachy four centuries earlier. "Wouldn't it be convenient," so the thinking went, "if Malachy's prophecies just happened to predict events the way we want them to turn out?"

It started when an ancient parchment was supposedly discovered in the Vatican archives in Rome. The discoverer was a Spanish scholar named Alphonsus Ciacconius, who was one of the world's leading experts in the dating of old manuscripts. He announced that the parchment, which bore a series of cryptic phrases in Latin, originated in the middle of the 12th century – just the time that Saint Malachy was supposed to have written his prophecy down.

With the help of another scholar, Ciacconius managed to decipher the manuscript. The seemingly cryptic Latin phrases constituted a list of all the Popes that would be elected after the time of Saint Malachy. There are no fewer than 112 Popes on the list, the first 74 of which corresponded fairly accurately to the actual Popes who had been elected prior the discovery of the manuscript. The Latin phrases can be interpreted as a verbal pun or metaphor on the name or birthplace of the Pope in question. For example, the fifth item on the list reads *De rure albo*. This literally means "from the white country" – but it can be taken as a pun on Albion, the ancient name for Britain. The fifth Pope after the time of Saint Malachy, Adrian IV, just happened to be the only British-born Pope.

As time went on, a problem became apparent. The new Popes who were elected after the discovery of the manuscript didn't fit the prophecies anything like as well as the earlier Popes. By the late 17th century the discrepancy had become painfully obvious, and a Catholic scholar named Louis Moréri realized that everything hinged on the year 1590. That was the year that Ciacconius supposedly discovered the manuscript – and it was the year the prophecies switched from being accurate to inaccurate.

There was a succession of three different Popes in 1590. Sixtus V died in August to be replaced by Urban VII, who died the following month and was replaced by Gregory XIV. The prophecies for Sixtus V and Urban VII are good matches, but the prophecy for the next Pope didn't match Gregory XIV at all. Moréri realized this was the single most important prophecy in the whole list – all the rest were window dressing.

The key prophecy, for the Pope to follow Urban VII, reads *Ex antiquitate Urbis*. This means "of the old city", which doesn't make much sense in the context of Urban's actual successor, Gregory XIV. On the other hand, it's a perfect match for one of the other cardinals who was in the running – Girolamo Simoncelli, who was born in Orvieto. The Latin name for Orvieto is Urbevetanum, meaning "the old city". Simoncelli was the candidate favoured by the King of Spain, Philip II... who just happened to be the rich patron of Alphonsus Ciacconius. And Ciacconius, of course, just happened to be the scholar who discovered the prophecies and vouched for their authenticity! Moréri concluded that the Papal Prophecies were nothing but an audacious political gambit – albeit an unsuccessful one – to strengthen Simoncelli's claim to the Papacy.

Bonfires of vanity (1494)

After the fall of the Roman Empire in the 5th century, most of the progress made in ancient times was lost to Europe. The continent fell back into a state of ignorance, superstition and hand-to-mouth existence – and things didn't begin to improve until the 14th and 15th centuries. This period is called the Renaissance, from a French word meaning "rebirth". One of its main centres was the Italian city-state of Florence, which saw a revival of skills in a whole range of areas from philosophy to engineering. Most of all, though, the Florentine Renaissance is remembered for its works of art – Michelangelo, Leonardo da Vinci and Botticelli were all products of the period.

At its height, Florence was ruled by members of the Medici family, who enthusiastically promoted Renaissance values. In the late 15th century, Lorenzo de' Medici – Lorenzo the Magnificent – became one of the greatest patrons of art in history. Under his sponsorship, painters like Botticelli were encouraged to depict the gods and goddesses of ancient mythology – the first non-Christian art that Europe had seen since the days of the Roman Empire.

Not everyone was a fan of the Renaissance, however. In the 1490s, Lorenzo's rule was challenged by a religious extremist named Girolamo Savonarola – who loudly denounced anything with a hint of ancient Greece or Rome about it. Savonarola was a friar from a humble family – he didn't live in a huge palace like the Medicis, but in an austere monk's cell. Although he was a Catholic – the Protestant Reformation was still in the future – Savonarola's mind worked like the purest of Puritans. He couldn't stand to see other people enjoying themselves, and he believed the end-times were imminent. It was true the world hadn't ended in the year 1000, as the Bible seemed to imply it would – but there was another roundish number just a few years away. Savonarola put his money on 1500.

Savonarola informed the people of Florence that there was still time to repent their evil ways. He was a slick talker, and people listened to him. By 1494 the Medicis had been kicked out, and Savonarola – still living in his humble monk's cell – was effectively the ruler of Florence. Under the Medicis it had been the most forward-looking city in the world – under its new leader it became the most backward-looking. Savonarola set out to undo the Renaissance.

He organised a series of communal book-burnings called "Bonfires of Vanity". It wasn't just books that were thrown into the flames – anything that would burn could go on the bonfire, as long as it wasn't Christian. Botticelli gathered together all the pagan-themed paintings he had produced – the ones he could get his hands on – and threw them into the fire. Fortunately a few escaped, such as his famous portrayal of the Birth of Venus... but from that time onwards Botticelli restricted his output to pious Christian imagery.

Savonarola's extremism was viewed with alarm by those higher up in the Church. In 1497 he was excommunicated by the Pope, who went on to threaten the entire population of Florence with a similar fate if they didn't do something about him. The Florentines decided to take a pragmatic approach, and they executed Savonarola as a heretic on 23 May 1498. A few years later, the Medici were in power again and the Renaissance was back on course.

Phantom time (1000)

British readers will be well aware that, in parts of the country at least, it's difficult to dig in the ground without finding traces of the Roman occupation. It may be the remains of a villa, complete with central heating and neatly tiled bathrooms, but more likely it will be a few low value coins. But in either case, it constitutes hard evidence that the Roman Empire really did exist. On the continent the evidence is even more striking, with buildings and engineering works still standing for anyone to see. In Rome itself, the Pantheon and the Colosseum are among the most impressive buildings in Europe.

It's the same with the written word. Thousands of books and documents survive from the Roman period, whether they're the work of poets like Ovid and Virgil, historians like Livy and Tacitus or politicians like Cicero and Julius Caesar. Across the whole gamut of human creativity, the story is the same. Whether you're talking about literature, or art, or science, or engineering, or architecture, or politics, or economics – there's no doubt the Roman Empire existed.

When it comes to the period following the fall of the Roman Empire, it's a different matter altogether. There are no great buildings, no aqueducts, no marble sculptures, no centrally-heated bathrooms. You can dig for years without finding a single coin with a date on it between the 7th and 10th centuries. Writings from the period are few and far between, and often only exist in later copies. Hard evidence for the "Early Middle Ages", as the period is known to historians, is in short supply. You have to take it as a matter of faith.

Or do you? A radical alternative has been suggested by some German scholars – that the Early Middle Ages never existed. According to the Phantom Time Hypothesis, as it's known, the whole period was deliberately fabricated by a small number of government officials. If true, the exercise would probably qualify as the most grandiose, audacious – and successful – conspiracy in history.

According to the theory, the instigator of the conspiracy was the Holy Roman Emperor Otto III. In terms of conventional history, he reigned between the years 980 and 1002. For a devoutly Christian Emperor, this was a significant moment in history – spanning the thousandth anniversary of the appearance of the Son of God. But was it really the thousandth anniversary?

Proponents of the Phantom Time Hypothesis believe that Otto actually became Emperor something like 680 years after Christ, not 980 years. He then got his scribes to fabricate three centuries worth of fake history to make it look like it was 300 years later than it was. This explains why there is so little archaeological evidence dating from the "phantom" centuries, and why the architectural style of the 11th century is so little advanced on that of the 7th.

Appealing as it is, the Phantom Time Hypothesis doesn't hold water. There is strong evidence from other cultures – China, India and the Islamic world – that the phantom centuries really did exist. In other words, they're a purely European phenomenon. The sad fact is that, during those centuries, Europe was an insignificant backwater of civilization.

The first spin-doctors (1274 BC)

One of the earliest recorded battles in history took place in 1274 BC, between an Egyptian army led by Pharaoh Ramesses II and forces of the rival Hittite Empire, centred in modern-day Turkey. The battle was fought at a place called Kadesh, in what is now Syria. For many years the Battle of Kadesh was only known to historians from Egyptian writings, which portrayed it as a massive victory for Ramesses II.

Starting in the 19th century, new archaeological discoveries began to paint a different picture. The Hittites' own records of the battle were found, in which they put their own spin on events. According to the Hittite account they were the true victors, and the Egyptians had been forced into retreat.

Perhaps the most accurate version of events, however, comes from a Peace Treaty the two sides agreed to sign after the battle. This makes it clear that neither side won. They both emerged from the battle in exactly the same position they had entered it – and the treaty ensured they would stay in that position!

The battle that changed history (778)

In the 8th century, France was a Christian country and Spain was an Islamic one. But that's not to say that either country was united. Spain was split between two rival Caliphates – the Umayyads and the Abbasids. France was gradually being absorbed into Charlemagne's empire, but there were still parts of the south-west that had not been conquered.

Of the two rival factions in Spain, the Abbasids were in the weaker position – and they knew it. From their point of view, an alliance with Charlemagne made a lot of sense. An alliance made sense to Charlemagne too, because it would strengthen his position in the south-west. It was agreed that Charlemagne's forces would march to the Abbasid-held city of Zaragoza where they would help their new allies fight off the Umayyads.

It didn't work out that way. When Charlemagne's army arrived in Zaragoza, they discovered there was disagreement among the Abbasids as to how to proceed. Eventually Charlemagne was told his aid wasn't required after all – although he was given a large quantity of gold by way of compensation.

Charlemagne's army headed back to France, crossing the Pyrenees by way of a narrow mountain pass at Roncevaux. The forward part of the army, led by the Emperor himself, made it through safely. But as the baggage train – complete with its golden treasure – was passing through on the evening of 15 August 778, it was ambushed by Basque fighters. The attackers had no political objectives – they were simply after the gold. In the narrow confines of the pass, the army's rearguard – led by a man named Roland – was no match for the marauding locals. Roland was killed, his soldiers suffered massive casualties, and the attackers slipped off into the night carrying their ill-gotten gains.

The Battle of Roncevaux Pass is seen as one of the great turning points of history. This isn't because of the battle itself – which was simply an ambush by well-armed bandits – but because of its consequences. The Christian Emperor Charlemagne wanted to form an alliance with Islamic Spain. After the fiasco of Roncevaux Pass he changed his mind. From that point on, Europe had its first Iron Curtain... not between Capitalism and Communism, but between Christianity and Islam.

By the time of the Crusades, more than three hundred years later, people had forgotten the two sides had ever been on speaking terms with each other. The Battle of Roncevaux Pass became romanticized as the first great clash between Christianity and Islam – something that simply wasn't the case. The Basque bandits who slaughtered Roland and his men were Christians, not Muslims.

The *Song of Roland*, dating from the late 12th century, is one of the earliest works of French literature. It tells the story of Roncevaux Pass – not the way it happened, but the way the French wanted it to happen. Roland is portrayed as Charlemagne's greatest general, who dies a hero's death fighting the "Islamic" foe. In retaliation, Charlemagne's forces hit back at the Muslims and inflict a crushing defeat on them – an event that never actually took place.

A forgotten Pharaoh (1334 BC)

Amenhotep IV became Pharaoh of Egypt in 1351 BC, inheriting the title from his father Amenhotep III. The name "Amenhotep" is a tribute to Amun-Ra, the most popular of the many Egyptian gods of the time. All priests were powerful in ancient Egypt, but the priests of Amun-Ra were the most powerful of all.

Most Pharaohs, before and after Amenhotep IV, were content to accept the fact that priests had almost as much power and influence as they did themselves. But young Amenhotep was different. Soon after he became Pharaoh, he made all the priests redundant. He set about eradicating all references to Amun-Ra, and replacing them with the name of a new deity – the Aten. The Aten was represented as a Sun-disk – as far superior to the other gods as the Sun was superior to the stars. Aten-worship became mandatory, while worship of other gods was outlawed.

The Pharaoh changed his name to Akhenaten in honour of the new god, and moved his capital from Thebes to a new city 400 kilometres away called Akhetaten. The new capital was filled with images of the Aten – and of Akhenaten himself, who was the Aten's living prophet on Earth.

At this distance in time, Akhenaten's motives are unclear. Some people see him as an enlightened religious reformer who was centuries ahead of his time – a forerunner of the monotheistic religions of today. Others see him as a cynical megalomaniac who swept away the old religion in order to consolidate his own power-base. Of the two views, the second was more prevalent among his contemporaries.

Akhenaten ruled Egypt for 17 years. After his death in 1334 BC, it's likely that he was succeeded for a short time by one of his wives who attempted to keep the new religion going. But within two years, Akhenaten's young son was on the throne. It was still less than 20 years since Akhenaten had dismissed the priests of the old religion. Many of them were still alive –and they wanted their jobs back. They set to work bending the ear of the new Pharaoh.

The pharaoh Akhenaten worships the Aten disk with his wife and children.

Akhenaten had called his son Tutankhaten, but under pressure from the Amun-Re worshippers the young Pharaoh changed it to Tutankhamun. He reinstated the old religions, and moved the capital back from Akhetaten to Thebes. This was just the beginning, though – Tutankhamun's successors went even further. We've already seen, in Chapter 3, how they attempted to delete Tutankhamun from the historical record after his death. They wanted to do the same for Akhenaten, but that wasn't going to be easy. Tutankhamun's reign was short and relatively uneventful – the same could hardly be said for his father. To erase the memory of Akhenaten meant erasing a sizeable city, a fully worked-up religion and almost twenty years of history.

For the nation that built the pyramids, no task was too daunting to undertake. All visible traces of Akhenaten were obliterated, and for the next 3000 years he was lost to history. It was only when archaeologists started digging in the sands of Egypt in the 18th century that the truth about his existence became known.

Appendix

1334 BC: Death of the Egyptian Pharaoh Akhenaten, whose existence was subsequently erased from the historical record. [Chapter 8]

1323 BC: Death of Akhenaten's son Tutankhamun, who may have been the victim of assassination. [Chapter 3]

1274 BC: Battle of Kadesh, fought between the ancient Egyptians and the Hittite Empire. In their records of the battle, both sides claimed victory. [Chapter 8]

336 BC: Assassination of Philip II of Macedon, father of Alexander the Great. Soon afterwards, conspiracy theories arose linking Alexander to the murder. [Chapter 3]

186 BC: The Roman Senate outlaws the Bacchanalia – the secret gatherings of the Dionysian mystery cult. [Chapter 7]

80 BC: The Roman politician Cicero makes a speech that includes the phrase *cui bono*, meaning "who benefits?" – the heart of conspiracy thinking. [Chapter 1]

44 BC: Assassination of Julius Caesar by a group of rival politicians. [Chapter 1]

367: An uprising in Roman Britain which the historian Ammianus Marcellinus referred to as a "Barbarian Conspiracy". [Chapter 1]

778: The Battle of Roncevaux Pass, in which Charlemagne's army was attacked by Christian bandits. Later accounts turned the attackers into Islamic warriors. [Chapter 8]

1000: An important year for the Christian religion, which occurred during the reign of Holy Roman Emperor Otto III. But did he falsify historical records to make it appear that was the case? [Chapter 8]

1002: King Ethelred the Unready orders the St. Brice's Day Massacre – a solution to the Danish problem which ends up misfiring badly. [Chapter 4]

1079: Archbishop Stanislaus of Szczepanów is murdered in his cathedral by a scheming monarch, in a pre-echo of the Becket case 91 years later. [Chapter 4]

1100: Death of King William II in a hunting accident – although it may not have been an accident. [Chapter 5]

1120: The sinking of the White Ship kills the cream of young English nobility, including the heir to the throne. [Chapter 5]

1136: Geoffrey of Monmouth writes History of the Kings of Britain, the majority of which is fraudulent. [Chapter 8]

1170: Archbishop Thomas Becket is murdered in Canterbury Cathedral, apparently at the instigation of King Henry II. [Chapter 4]

1173: Two "green children" appear from nowhere outside a small English village, and go on to attract a disproportionate amount of attention from the authorities. [Chapter 6]

1192: King Conrad of Jerusalem is killed by hired assassins days after his election – but who hired them? [Chapter 3]

1307: Suppression of the Knights Templar, leading to one of history's most enduring mysteries. What did the Templars know that made them so dangerous? [Chapter 7]

1327: Death of Edward II, leaving England in the hands of his French wife and a scheming politician named Mortimer. [Chapter 3]

1407: Assassination of Duke Louis of Orléans on the orders of Duke John of Burgundy, who goes on to be assassinated himself 12 years later. [Chapter 3]

1441: Trial of Eleanor Duchess of Gloucester and her co-conspirators for "treasonable necromancy" – supposedly a plot to kill the king by witchcraft. [Chapter 7]

1471: King Henry VI is deposed, arrested, imprisoned... and then conveniently found dead in his cell. [Chapter 5]

1487: Rebellion against Henry VII in the name of a young boy, Lambert Simnel, whose supporters say is the rightful heir to the throne. [Chapter 6]

1494: A fanatical friar named Savonarola ousts the government of Florence and sets about a campaign of book-burning. [Chapter 8]

1497: Perkin Warbeck launches another rebellion against Henry VII, this time claiming to be King Richard IV. [Chapter 6]

1513: Niccolò Machiavelli writes The Prince, in which he promotes the idea that "the end justifies the means". [Chapter 4]

1587: Mary Queen of Scots is executed for treason, after agents posing as Catholics successfully draw her into a fabricated anti-government plot. [Chapter 2]

1590: A forged mediaeval document is "discovered" in the Vatican, with the intention of strengthening one particular cardinal's bid for the Papacy. [Chapter 8]

1592: Various prominent figures, including Sir Walter Raleigh and Christopher Marlowe, are accused of belonging to a subversive secret society called the School of Night. [Chapter 7]

1593: The playwright Christopher Marlowe is killed, supposedly in self-defence, by some of the same government agents who were involved in framing Mary Queen of Scots. [Chapter 5]

1604: Death of the Earl of Oxford, who some people believe wrote the plays normally attributed to William Shakespeare. [Chapter 6]

1605: The Gunpowder Plot by a group of Catholics to blow up the House of Lords. In the wake of the fake "Popish Plot" later in the 17th century, there were suggestions it might have been a similar attempt to discredit Catholics.
[Chapter 2]

1610: Assassination of Henri IV of France, which benefited his wife far more than it benefited the supposed perpetrator. [Chapter 3]

1612: Sudden death of Prince Henry Frederick, the heir to the English and Scottish thrones. Dismissed by modern historians as being due to natural causes, it was widely assumed to be poisoning at the time. [Chapter 5]

1616: Robert and Frances Carr are found guilty of murder, but pardoned by King James I. Was that because he was part of the murder plot? [Chapter 3]

1648: Parliament is taken over by the army, after "Pride's Purge" gets rid of all the moderate members. [Chapter 4]

1653: For six months, England is ruled by Praise-God Barebone and his Fifth Monarchists – a group of religious fanatics who believe the end-times are imminent. [Chapter 7]

1660: The Indemnity and Oblivion Act makes it a criminal offence to speak about the period between the execution of Charles I and the restoration of Charles II. [Chapter 8]

1669: The Man in the Iron Mask is arrested in France and held prisoner for the rest of his life. No-one ever discovers who he is or what his crime was. [Chapter 6]

1678: The Popish Plot is fabricated by a group of fanatical Protestants to make it look as though Catholics are conspiring against the government. [Chapter 2]

1745: The mysterious Count of Saint Germain appears in London, and subsequently in other cities around Europe. He wields considerable influence in high circles, although no-one knows who he is or where he comes from. [Chapter 6]

1762: Catherine the Great seizes power in Russia from her husband, Peter III. She then embarks on a systematic programme to blacken his reputation and justify her takeover of the country. [Chapter 5]

1776: A new secret society called the Illuminati is formed in Bavaria. It only survives in its original form for a few years, but its legacy in the shadowy world of conspiracy theories continues to this day. [Chapter 7]

1788: King Gustav III of Sweden contrives what would nowadays be called a "false flag operation", in order to start a war with Russia. [Chapter 2]

1791: Death of Mozart, two months after his opera The Magic Flute depicted secret Masonic-style rituals on stage. Was there any connection between the two events? [Chapter 7]

1792: Gustav III of Sweden is assassinated at a masked ball. When the Italian composer Verdi tried to turn the incident into an opera, it was vetoed as being too politically sensitive. [Chapter 3]

1812: Assassination of the British Prime Minister, Spencer Perceval. His assassin, who claimed to be acting alone, may have been subsidized by leading businessmen. [Chapter 3]

1821: Death of Napoleon in British custody. His doctor believed there was a systematic campaign to end the French Emperor's life – possibly by poisoning. [Chapter 5]

1828: Mysterious appearance of 17 year old Kaspar Hauser in Nuremberg. Although the boy had no idea who he was, rumours sprang up that he was the missing heir of the Grand Duke of Baden. [Chapter 6]

1839: The British invade Afghanistan, with the aim of ousting its pro-Russian ruler and installing a puppet leader of their own. The whole thing goes horribly wrong. [Chapter 4]

1851: Start of the bloodiest conflict the world has ever seen – the Taiping Rebellion in China. The leader of the rebellion claims to be the younger brother of Jesus Christ. [Chapter 6]

1865: Assassination of Abraham Lincoln. Was it a low-level conspiracy by disgruntled Southerners, as conventional historians have it, or a high-level conspiracy by the people who stood to gain most from Lincoln's death? [Chapter 3]

1870: The Prussian Prime Minister, Otto von Bismarck, subtly rewords a message from the Prussian king in order to provoke the French into starting the Franco-Prussian War. [Chapter 2]

1885: Reverend A. B. Grimaldi produces a genealogical table showing how Queen Victoria is descended from the Biblical kings of Judah. [Chapter 7]

1888: A series of brutal murders in London is attributed to a killer, "Jack the Ripper", who is never caught. Were the murders the work of a madman, or a member of the establishment who was silencing people who knew too much? [Chapter 6]

1898: A mysterious explosion sinks the USS Maine in Havana harbour, and within two months America is at war with Spain. Did the Americans sink their own ship as an excuse to start the war? [Chapter 2]

1902: "Accidental" death of Émile Zola, four years after he accused top-ranking members of the French Army of lying, falsifying evidence and covering up the true facts in the Dreyfus case. [Chapter 5]

1915: The British liner Lusitania is sunk by a German torpedo, killing over a hundred American passengers. Some people believe the ship was deliberately put at risk in order to draw the United States into the First World War. [Chapter 2]

1916: Murder of Rasputin, the most trusted advisor of the Russian Emperor. The fatal bullet appeared to be come from a British service revolver – but why did Britain want Rasputin dead? [Chapter 5]

1933: The burning of the German parliament building, the Reichstag, is blamed on Communists... but the head of the German government, Adolf Hitler, stood to gain more. [Chapter 2]

1935: An organization called Deutsches Ahnenerbe, or German Heritage, is set up by the SS to prove that Germany was the cradle of world civilization. [Chapter 8]

1939: The Nazis use false flag tactics to make it look like Polish insurgents are attacking German installations – thus paving the way for the German invasion of Poland and the start of the Second World War. [Chapter 2]

1940: Execution of Soviet official Nikolai Yezhov, who had been responsible for erasing hundreds of people from the historic record. In turn, Yezhov himself is erased. [Chapter 8]

1942: The Allies stage a major assault on the French coast, the Dieppe Raid, which ends in disastrous failure. Even if it had succeeded, the operation would have achieved nothing of military value. [Chapter 4]

1943: Death of Polish General Sikorski in an air crash. The circumstances of the accident had been described in an anonymous phone call six weeks earlier, leading to the suspicion that it was a "planned accident". [Chapter 5]

1946: The British Prime Minister hands over a state-of-the-art jet engine to the Soviet Union, allowing them to incorporate it in the MiG-15 fighter – which went on to be used against British pilots in the Korean War. [Chapter 4]

1948: An unidentified man is found dead on Somerton beach in Australia, with clues indicating that he was a secret service agent killed in the line of duty – but for which country, no-one knows. [Chapter 6]

1954: The leader of a "flying saucer cult" predicts the end of the world. When it fails to happen, the cult members become stronger believers than ever before – the first recorded case of Cognitive Dissonance. [Chapter 7]

1957: Britain conducts a series of massive H-bomb tests – or at least, that is how they are announced to the world. In fact, the explosions were much smaller than claimed, and their motivation was political rather than scientific. [Chapter 4]

1961: The CIA sponsors an armed invasion of Cuba, centred around the Bay of Pigs. It fails miserably. [Chapter 2]

1962: The CIA produces plans for further false flag operations against the Cubans, under the codename Operation Northwoods. [Chapter 2]

1963: President John F. Kennedy is assassinated in Dallas, in circumstances that have never adequately been explained. [Chapter 1]

1964: The United States uses the "Gulf of Tonkin incident" as an excuse to start the Vietnam War. But the incident – an unprovoked attack by the Vietnamese on US Navy ships – probably never took place. [Chapter 2]

1967: An eccentric Frenchman creates a hoax, involving an organization called the Priory of Sion, in order to support his claim to be the rightful king of France. [Chapter 7]

1974: A wealthy industrialist sponsors a ship, the Glomar Explorer, to retrieve manganese nodules from the deep ocean floor. In reality, the ship is operated by the CIA in an attempt to retrieve the wreck of a Soviet submarine. [Chapter 4]

1997: Death of Diana Princess of Wales in a road traffic accident. There have been persistent rumours that the "accident" was the work of the British secret service. [Chapter 1]

2001: A carefully planned terrorist attack destroys the World Trade Center in New York. But who planned it? Some people believe it was a false flag operation by the United States government. [Chapter 1]

2003: The invasion of Iraq is justified as the only way to destroy the country's chemical and biological weapons. But Iraq didn't have any such weapons – so what was the real motivation for the invasion? [Chapter 1]

Index